Harold T. Bryson

Portraits of God

Broadman Press
Nashville, Tennessee

To Raymond and Katie Bryson—
Parents who gave me a life.

To Tom and Nell Hearne—
People who gave me a wife.

4251-60
ISBN: 0-8054-5160-9

Dewey Decimal Classification: 231
Subject heading: GOD

Library of Congress Catalog Card Number: 77-82401
Printed in the United States of America

Foreword

I have known Harold Bryson since his high school days in Tupelo, Mississippi. I was privileged to share revival services on two occasions in his home church, the Harrisburg Baptist Church. As I recall, he had already committed his life to the gospel ministry, and was having a positive influence upon other high school age young people.

I have watched his progress with interest and gratitude to God. His training at New Orleans Baptist Theological Seminary culminated with the Doctor of Theology. During his school years he pastored churches in Mississippi.

Dr. Bryson was one of the first persons added to the faculty after I came to New Orleans Baptist Theological Seminary to be president. We were attracted to him as a potential faculty member because of his academic training, his proven competence in pastoral ministries, and his writing ability. Along with a warm, outgoing personality, and a family equally committed to Jesus Christ, Dr. Bryson has proven to be a providential choice and he has become one of our most popular professors.

This present volume will give evidence of his homiletical skills, his love for the Word of God, and his lucid, intriguing style of writing. All this combines to make this book an attractive addition to the library of any Christian.

—Dr. Landrum P. Leavell, II, President,
NEW ORLEANS BAPTIST THEOLOGICAL SEMINARY

Preface

Little Sarah, a six-year-old, sat at her desk drawing on her new sketch pad. Her mother passed by the room and saw Sarah engrossed in her work. "What are you drawing?" the mother asked. Sarah quickly responded, "I am drawing a picture of God."

The mother hesitated a moment from shock. Then she ventured, "Sarah, no one can draw God's picture. No one knows what God looks like." Sarah continued with her drawings as she mused. Then she said, "Mother, they'll know what God looks like when I get through."

Through the years people have longed to know the nature and character of God. The ancient patriarch Job wanted to learn about God. "Oh that I knew where I might find him! that I might come even to his seat!" (Job 23:3). God obliged Job's desire and revealed himself in some unusual pictures. God appeared in a whirlwind and disclosed the mighty works of creation. Philip, the Lord's apostle, expressed a desire to see God. "Lord, shew us the Father, and it sufficeth us" (John 14:8). Jesus pointed to himself, "He that hath seen me hath seen the Father" (John 14:9). God revealed himself in a person. If you want a portrait of God, look at Jesus. No one needs to be confused or frustrated about the nature and character of God. If you want to see some portraits of God, look at the various poses of Jesus which the gospels portray.

Technically, biblical photography is called general and special revelation. General revelation means that God has photographed himself in nature, history, and human life. Special revelation refers to pictures of God in the mighty acts of Israel's history and above all in Jesus Christ.

The Bible is the technical name for the photograph album. The Lord has spoken and acted, and the Bible holds these unique snapshots. God allowed the pictures of himself to be much clearer with the passing of years. God's pictures of himself can be seen in earliest photography framed in the Old Testament. As history unfolded, God gave pictures with a sharper focus. Technically, this would be called "progressive revelation" by the theologians. It means that God gave pictures of himself only as man could understand and interpret them.

The latest and greatest portraits of God are those disclosed by Jesus Christ. The life of Jesus gave a unique disclosure of the divine hiddenness. It is a visual commentary of the unseen God. This means that Jesus gives us the greatest portraits of God. He gave dramatic visibility to the features of God photographed in the Old Testament. Therefore, if you want an authentic, lifelike portrait of God, look at Jesus Christ.

To satisfy some human curiosities about God, some have ignored biblical portraits of God. They chose to draw their own caricatures of God. This means the drawings are ludicrous exaggerations. Some caricatures blow up some features of God's nature. You have seen such enlargements of God as a capricious deity rather touchy and somewhat irritable. From this drawing you get an idea of God as a trickster who wishes to harm mankind. Blowups in photography are burlesque exaggerations. These distortions depict God as a capricious deity, loving some people, hating some, ignoring others, according to the whim of the moment. This drawing often depicts a god sneaking around spying, trying to catch someone doing bad so he can punish them.

The parodies of God as the Great Grandfather or the Great

Computer do not need circulation. These are grotesque distortions of a deity who answers all questions, solves all problems, protects from all hurt, makes life comfortable, and gets people out of trouble. Also, the caricature of God as the Feudal Boss shows a divine being whose honor has been offended, and his satisfaction must be demanded.

Some describe the reality of God with abstract academic information. Actually these are not pictures but flash cards with words. Mentioning words such as immortality, omniscience, omnipotence, providence, wisdom, power, righteousness, justice, goodness, and truth do not give an adequate picture of a loving, active, personal God. Albert Knudson spoke of these attributes as "something like pins stuck in a cushion."[1]

The more you listen to what others say about God, the more you become aware of human feelings about God. Some mental snapshots suffer from an overexposure. Some have allowed too much human light to come in and distort the picture. Allowing too much of God's sovereignty distorts the feature of God giving people freedom. Also, allowing too much human sentimentalism into God's picture distorts the just judgment of God on sin. Without a doubt the lens have been opened too wide and God's wrath has been overexposed and God's mercy and grace has been distorted. Or the lens could have been opened too wide the other way and neglected the justice of God. This would characterize the Lord as the negligent parent who fails to discipline.

Human caricatures will not suffice for portraits of God. The Bible contains the most interesting and profitable snapshots of God. It is the picture album God has authorized for a genuine portrait of his features and his ways. People's interest in God, the distorted ideas of God, and my personal desire to know more about God prompted me to go through the Bible and collect some of my favorite portraits of God. This book represents a journey through the gospel narratives in order to see various disclosures of God. The more I looked, the more pictures of God I saw revealed in Jesus Christ. Therefore, I had to be selective with the portraits and pick my favorite poses. Other people might chose other poses. I intend for this book to be a "look-along" adventure. I would like for you to sit down with me, and look at my collection of God's portraits from the Great Album. It may be possible for me to call to your attention some features of God's character you have not seen before.

I am deeply grateful for people who put the first pictures of God in my album. Parents gave me a picture of God who loved, cared, and shared life with me. Seminary professors helped me to get God in biblical focus. These professors who taught me are now my colleagues at New Orleans Baptist Theological Seminary. I continue to be grateful for their help. They continue to help me get God in focus academically. But even greater than their scholarship, I see the reflection of God in their daily lives.

My secretary at New Orleans Baptist Theological Seminary, Miss Kathryn Harper, deserves a special commendation with regard to this book. She typed the original draft from my almost undecipherable handwriting. She possessed proficiency in typing, and she manifested a gracious spirit with numerous retypes, deadlines, and unusual idiosyncrasies of this author.

My wife, Judy, has always been interested in looking at my collection of God's portraits. She has looked with interest and listened with patience. She has been especially helpful in the assimilation of this album. William and Thomas, our two sons, have started collecting their pictures of God. Often I want to hand them a "ready-made" album. But I realize that they need to select for themselves. I sincerely hope that by our precept and example we can help them to put biblical portraits of God into their albums rather than human caricatures.

Contents

1.
The Good Shepherd

Since I was a boy, I have thoroughly disliked having my picture taken. It was not that it hurt, but every time I posed for a picture, the photographer would say. "Try to be natural." After a photographer would tell me to be natural my posture would stiffen, my countenance would be artificial, and my smile would be a forced, superficial grin. It is hard to be unaffected after someone says, "Be natural!"

God wants people to see his real nature. When God poses for pictures, he is always natural. God continues to be what he has always been. The picture of God as Good Shepherd is one of his first pictures. God wanted people to see the expression of his countenance, the smile on his face after finding a sheep, and his feelings toward wandering humanity. God used the figure of the shepherd and the sheep to give a glimpse of his feelings toward humanity.

The Old Testament picture takers spoke of God in terms of a shepherd. The psalmist said, "The Lord is my shepherd" (Ps. 23:1). "Thou leadest thy people like a flock by the hand of Moses and Aaron" (Ps. 77:20). "For he is our God; and we are the people of his pasture, and the sheep of his hand" (Ps. 95:7).

Isaiah pictured God as a gentle and loving shepherd. "He shall feed his flock like a shepherd: he shall gather the lambs with his arm, and carry them in his bosom, and shall gently lead those that are with young" (Isa. 40:11). Jeremiah pictured God as a shepherd seeking sheep that had gone astray.

"And I will gather the remnant of my flock out of all countries whither I have driven them, and will bring them again to their folds; and they shall be fruitful and increase. And I will set up shepherds over them which shall feed them" (Jer. 23:3–4). Ezekiel's concept of God was one of a seeking shepherd. "Behold, I, even I, will both search my sheep, and seek them out. I will feed them in a good pasture, and upon the high mountains of Israel shall their fold be" (Ezek. 34:11,14).

God's photograph of his shepherd nature came into more distinct focus in Jesus. He gave the world a beautiful picture of God when he told the story of the shepherd with a hundred sheep. As the shepherd counted the sheep at the close of the day, he noticed that one sheep was missing. Feeling concern for the lost animal, the shepherd left ninety-nine other sheep to search for the one that was lost. He went over mountains and hills, valleys and ravines, cliffs and crags to seek a lost sheep. When the shepherd found the animal, he laid it gently on his shoulder and brought it back to the fold.

The simple story of the shepherd searching for a strayed sheep furnishes one of the clearest and sharpest pictures of God in the gospels. To see the full beauty of this picture of God we can look at it constantly and turn it at different angles. There is more in this simple picture than meets the eye.

God Values

As we look at the picture of God in this simple story, we see the value a shepherd placed on one sheep. Jesus told the story of a man who had a hundred sheep. Bible scholars make a note of this facet of the story. The normal flock of a shepherd was one-third this amount. Fifty sheep would have been an enormous flock. Probably Jesus used this figure to teach a truth to the scribes and Pharisees. These two groups sought to discredit the ministry of Jesus. The occasion of this story and the other two following ones (lost coin and loving father) came as a result of their criticism of Jesus eating with publicans and sinners.

Jesus stressed the fact that the man had a hundred sheep. He further emphasized that one sheep was lost. Probably the natural reaction of his critics was, "Let that strayed sheep go! You still have ninety-nine!" But a good shepherd did not look upon his sheep that way. Every sheep was valued by the shepherd. The shepherd was not content to dismiss the strayed animal or to place a greater importance upon the other sheep. The picture portrayed by the story becomes explicit. Jesus, the Good Shepherd, teaches that God values every person. Self-righteous scribes and Pharisees and un-righteous publicans and sinners have value to God. God values every person.

God's value of people can be seen in his knowledge of them. One amazing fact portrayed in the picture is that the shepherd knew each sheep. He knew that one was absent from the hundred. The fact that God values individual life may seem incredible in view of the vastness of the stellar universe. The psalmist expressed a problem at this point. "When I consider thy heavens, the work of thy fingers, the moon and the stars, which thou hast ordained; What is man, that thou art mindful of him? and the son of man, that thou visitest him?" (Ps. 8:3–4). Alfred Lord Tennyson pictured human beings as but "a trouble of ants in the gleam of a million, million suns." The psalmist recognized that though man may be physically small, he has supreme value. "For thou hast made him a little lower than the angels, and hast crowned him with glory and honour" (Ps. 8:5).

Even though there is a physical immensity to the uni-verse, human beings need not fear their value in God's sight. The star called Antares is big enough to contain without undue crowding some ninety million suns the size of ours.

But if, thinking of such vastness, we are moved to ask, "What value does one human being have in the light of all that vastness?" The answer to the question is: Man is a living soul, whereas Antares is nothing more than incandescent gas; and we may well believe that in the eyes of God lifeless stars and empty spaces, however vast, count for less than one little child.

The fact that God knows each person may be challenged not only by the immense size of the heavens but also by the human population of the earth. The world population comprises billions of people. On the freeway it seems that one-fourth of the world population is in front of me. Often we ask, "Does God really know every single human being?" The answer comes from the psalmist, "O Lord, thou hast searched me, and known me. Thou knowest my downsitting and mine uprising, thou understandest my thought afar off. Thou compassest my path and my lying down, and art acquainted with all my ways" (Ps. 139:1–3). God's power of knowing has a different dimension than ours. He knows our names. He knows our needs.

The fact that God values each sheep is clearly seen in his concern for the one lost sheep. When one sheep did not show, the shepherd went to look for it. He could have dismissed this particular sheep from his mind. The shepherd did not say, "I have ninety-nine left" and then forget the lost lamb. He was not satisfied with the percentage game. Could a mother with three children forget one? No, the central stress in the story of the shepherd and the sheep is on "one." It pictures God as deeming everyone precious in his sight. Any particular sheep could have strayed, and the shepherd would have looked. This was not a special sheep. It was one, and he gave attention to each one.

Our civilization often reduces an individual to an anonymous digit. Totalitarian movements major on the majority. Factories look upon human beings as "hands" adjunct to machines. But the picture of God portrays individual concern. The Good Shepherd is concerned for one sheep.

Each human being is a distinctive person. He is not a copy of his parents. He is uniquely different from any person who ever lived. Each person comes equipped with his own distinctive set of fingerprints, accent of voice, and turn of disposition.

Newspapers report the importance or value of one life in the search for a lost child, a missing aviator, or a person lost at sea. We know that each life is important. An inferiority complex should never belong to a human being. God deems each individual as a person of worth. This does not mean conceit or a superiority complex. Rather, it is the conviction that the person has abiding worth and value.

God Identifies

Continuing to look at the picture of God in the story of the lost sheep, we see another angle of God's nature. Notice the identity of the shepherd with the sheep. He leaves the ninety-nine in safety. He goes after the lost sheep. He searches until he finds the sheep. The word "until" tells of the unwearying persistence of the shepherd. In this angle of the photograph we see a seeking God. The illustration tells what God will do to find a human being.

The search of the shepherd gives the fact that God takes the initiative to search for erring human beings. The shepherd did not reason, "That sheep knows the way. He can get back by himself." No, the shepherd left the other sheep to search for the lost one himself. God takes the initiative, not waiting for us to come to our senses. Wandering humanity does not organize their thoughts and search for God. When the idea of the need for God comes to them, they are aware that God has been searching for them all along.

God pursues lost people. Often people picture God as a tyrant who makes people come to him in lowly submission.

God is not like Sergeant Friday, or Cannon, or Barnaby Jones, seeking a fugitive from the law. He is a loving God portrayed in the imagery of a gentle, seeking shepherd. Francis Thompson was once a fugitive from God. He was reared in a religious home. He studied for the priesthood, and then medicine, but each time he failed through a lack of interest and laziness. During his youth he became hooked on narcotics which all but destroyed him. As a young man, he picked up various jobs on London streets, blacking boots, selling matches, or holding horses. He would do anything that would help him buy a "fix." About the only decent thing Thompson did was to write poetry. On an impulse he sent some of the poems to Wilfred Meynell, an editor and publisher. He saw signs of a genius in Thompson. Meynell searched for the young poet. They found him in pitiable surroundings. They drew him from these conditions and rescued him for the enrichment of the world through English literature.

Francis Thompson saw the picture of God. He came to realize that even though he eluded the pursuit of people, he could not escape the pursuing love of God.

God is not like a policeman tracking a fleeing criminal, pursuing him through alleys and deserted buildings, so that he can arrest him and incarcerate him. Our God is like a shepherd who goes in search for a single stray. When he finds the lost sheep, he cradles it tenderly in his arms. He brings us to where we belong.

The search of the shepherd portrays the reality that God suffers to search and to rescue strayed human beings. Alfred Soord has a fine picture of a shepherd poised dangerously on a precipitous mountain slope, gathering in the lost sheep with a downward sweep of a strong arm. Soord's picture depicts an animal who has strayed stubbornly away from the care of the shepherd. The picture also depicts the truth that the Good Shepherd risks his life to rescue strayed sheep.

A good shepherd did more than merely search for sheep. Often he hazarded his life for the sheep, and on some occasions he had to lay down his life for the sheep. This especially happened when thieves or robbers came to despoil the flock. W. M. Thomson in *The Land and the Book* tells about actual accounts of shepherds who laid down their lives in death defending their flock.

Jesus laid down his life for every lost person. "I am the good shepherd; the good shepherd giveth his life for the sheep" (John 10:11). The picture of God searching for strayed human beings is enlarged and magnified at the place called Calvary. When Jesus died on the cross, he laid down his life for all people. Jesus gave a dramatic visibility to what God has always been. The Old Testament pictured God as one who identified sacrificially with his people. No picture of God is more vivid than the gospel account of the Son of God being led to the place of crucifixion. Jesus died. He laid down his life for straying human beings.

God Restores

Looking at the picture of God in the gospels as a shepherd seeking a lost sheep produces marvelous dividends. Now we see another interesting facet of the picture. After the shepherd finds the lost sheep, he places it upon his shoulder caressing it gently as he makes his way back to the sheepfold. Upon returning the shepherd calls for rejoicing. This suggests that God rejoices over people who have been found.

Several flocks of sheep often grazed together. There would be several shepherds in charge. Those whose flocks were safe would arrive home on time and bring news that one shepherd was still on the mountainside searching for a sheep which was lost. The whole village might watch anxiously. When they saw the shepherd returning with the lost sheep across his shoulders, they would celebrate.

The rejoicing of the shepherd gives us a glimpse into what makes God happy. Often the authentic picture of God gets blurred at this point. We have a tendency to think that God loves us on the basis of our merits. The scribes and Pharisees pictured God as one who would be happy when you fulfilled and obeyed hundreds of rules and regulations. These religious people could never be sure that God was really happy.

The prophet Micah struggled with what would please God. "Wherewith shall I come before the Lord, and bow myself before the high God? Shall I come before him with burnt offerings, with calves of a year old? Will the Lord be pleased with thousands of rams, or with ten thousands of rivers of oil? Shall I give my firstborn for my transgression, the fruit of my body for the sin of my soul? He hath showed thee, O man, what is good; and what doth the Lord require of thee, but to do justly, and to love mercy, and to walk humbly with thy God?" (Micah 6:6–8). According to Micah rituals did not please God. What makes God happy is a relationship with him. God wants a close fellowship with human beings. He will go to the greatest lengths in bringing humanity back to him.

The rejoicing of the shepherd also gives an insight into why God rejoices. The shepherd rejoiced because a potential disaster was averted. A robber could have stolen the sheep, or a wild animal could have killed the sheep. The shepherd and the village people rejoiced because a sheep was recovered. God rejoices when a human being yields to him. Consider the possibilities that can happen to human beings when they stray from the Good Shepherd. Because of their stubborn refusal to follow the leadership of the divine shepherd, they find themselves in unfamiliar territory and in extreme danger.

The word used to describe humanity's condition is "lost." Jesus used the word to mean a person who has lost his direction in life. Like the sheep in the wilderness, he is living a wandering, aimless, drifting life. A person is lost when he has lost his direction, when his life is a succession of thoughts and actions which are not directed to the true end of life or controlled by a right purpose. A person's "lostness" is determined by the direction he goes. Going away from God results in lostness. Turning to God in faith indicates meaning and significance as well as a final destination. Continuing to go away from the Good Shepherd results in destruction.

God rejoices when a person is found. With the shepherd, we are safe. Not only does it mean destruction to go against God, but it also means loneliness, or a lack of meaningful relationships. The Good Shepherd brings wandering sheep back into wholeness and meaningful relationships with others. The shepherd brought the sheep back to the flock. The sheep's worth was restored and the relationship with the flock restored. God rejoices when a sinner returns, for not only is the person restored within himself but is restored also in a meaningful relationship to others. One does not need to live a life wandering aimlessly. People need relationships with others. Apart from the relationship with the Good Shepherd there can be no genuine, meaningful relationship with others.

Now you have a treasured photograph of God in the likeness of a shepherd searching and recovering a lost sheep. Any other idea of God other than a positive, seeking love is unlike God and hence a human caricature.

2.
The Timekeeper

All during my lifetime I have had numerous questions about the nature and character of God. One prominent question that has puzzled me is, "Where did God come from?" My parents say that I asked them that question on several occasions. My children have asked me about the origin of God. Humanly speaking, I can neither comprehend nor explain the idea that God has no beginning, and he has no end. In my finiteness everyone and everything is measured in the realm of time. In my thinking everything must have a beginning, and everything must have a conclusion.

A close look into the gospel records of Jesus' life and ministry yields an interesting snapshot. It is the picture of God as The Timekeeper. Seeing God as the timekeeper can help us with our questions regarding the origin of God. All through the gospels we see snapshot after snapshot about the timelessness of God. Once as Jesus spoke to a group of Jews, he made a staggering statement: "Before Abraham was, I am" (John 8:58). Jesus said that God is the timekeeper. He revealed that God is the only person who is above and beyond time, and who can always say, "I am." God is the same yesterday, today, and forever. He is the God of Abraham and of Isaac and of Jacob. He is the God of people in our time. He is the God who will be after time. In Jesus the eternal God showed himself as the timekeeper.

God Starts Time

Go back as far as you can and think about time. When did

time begin? Many people have tried to explain the origin of time. There seems to be no more logical explanation than the truth that God, the Almighty Creator of the universe, started time. The origin of what we know as chronological time is stated in Genesis 1:1. "In the beginning God created the heaven and the earth." On the fourth day God said, "Let there be lights in the firmament of the heaven to divide the day from the night; and let them be for signs, and for seasons, and for days, and years" (Gen. 1:14). This is the biblical explanation about the origin of time. God thought of having days, nights, years, and seasons. Any measurement of time by man would be an investigation into this natural phenomenon which God started.

God created the uniqueness of time. He made it out of nothing. It is so unique that we cannot define it. We may be able to tell the time, but we cannot give a precise definition of time. We sense its passing in our consciousness. We measure its progress with delicately adjusted instruments. We mark its flight and read the record it leaves behind. William Marsden wrote: "What is time? The shadow on the dial, the striking of the clock, the running of the sand, day and night, summer and winter, months, years, centuries—these are but arbitrary outward signs, the measure of time, not time itself." [1]

There are various explanations of time. Modern science attempts to define time. Sometimes it is described in terms of mathematical formulas, sometimes by the analysis of dreams, and sometimes as a fourth dimension added to space. The Bible uses various words to describe the phenomenon of time: *kairos*, *aiōn*, and *chronos*. The characteristic thing about *kairos* is that it has to do with a definite point of time. *Aiōn* designates a duration of time. The word *chronos* refers to seasons or ages within history. The terminology of the New Testament teaches that "time in its unending extension as well as in its individual periods and moments is given by God and ruled by God." [2]

Time is so unique that it can be measured in many ways. Nicholas Berdyaev categorizes time into three sorts: cosmic, historical, and existential. He says cosmic time is measured with calendars, clocks, and other mathematical devices. Historical time is likewise calculated in terms of decades, centuries, and millenniums. Berdyaev gives a third kind as existential. It is characterized by intensity of experience.[3] Irrespective of what anyone says about time, the definition cannot describe it fully.

Because God created time, he controls it. If God created time, surely he can be sovereign over it and control it. Jesus said, "I am Alpha and Omega, the beginning and the end, the first and the last" (Rev. 22:13). The terms *alpha* and *omega* describe the great sovereignty of God in time. *Alpha* is the first letter of the Greek alphabet and *omega* is the last. This would say that from the beginning of recorded time until the end of recorded time God has been acting. He acted in previous years, he acts today, and he will go on acting even after history is ended.

The word beginning is *archē* and the word for end is *telos*. *Archē* can mean the beginning in point of time and *telos* can mean an end in a point of time. This teaches us that God existed before the world began and will be even after the world is ended. *Archē* can also mean source or origin, and *telos* can mean the consummation. This would suggest that Jesus Christ is the source of life and he is the goal toward which all of life moves.

Because God is supreme over time, he transcends all its limitations. God has no beginning or end. He is free from the succession of time, being the cause of the phenomenon we call time. When God calls himself the "I am" God, he uses a name involving eternity (Ex. 3:14).

God is not conditioned to the factor of time. He is not under the law of time. God is above time and space. God can see time past, present, and future as one eternal now. Time had to be God's idea.

God Visits Time

After God created time, he did not retire and watch its passing from heaven. He refused to become a passive spectator. God has been involved in time from its earliest beginnings, and he will always be deeply involved. God is active in the affairs of the world today. He is the main actor in the drama of human history.

God visited humanity from the beginning. A lively sense of the presence of God runs through the Old Testament from beginning to end. When the first human beings walked on earth, God was present. "And they heard the voice of the Lord God walking in the garden in the cool of the day: and Adam and his wife hid themselves from the presence of the Lord God amongst the trees of the garden" (Gen. 3:8). Whatever else this verse may teach, it definitely teaches us of the presence of God among his creation.

Throughout human history God has desired to make his presence known to all people. To accomplish this purpose, the Lord chose Abraham to make a great nation. God was present in a unique way with this nation so they could represent God to the rest of the nations. All the descendants of Abraham through Isaac and Jacob, known as Hebrews, constitute the nation through whom God revealed himself. God chose to be with Israel.

God assured Israel periodically of his unique presence with them. "And the Lord appeared unto Abram, and said, 'Unto thy seed will I give this land:' and there builded he an altar unto the Lord, who appeared unto him" (Gen. 12:7). God visited Abraham, Isaac, Jacob, and Joseph. During the plight of Jacob's children in Egypt, God promised to deliver them. "And I am come down to deliver them out of the hand of the Egyptians" (Ex. 3:8). They were assured of God's presence with the pillar of cloud by day and the pillar of fire by night. The Israelites acknowledged the presence of God with the construction of the tabernacle. Hundreds of years after the building of the tabernacle, the Israelites constructed a temple.

As we trace Israel's history, we see that the people were constantly aware of God's presence. There was despair among some after the destruction of the Temple in B.C. by Nebuchadnezzar. Ezekiel and others spoke of the glory of God or his presence in Babylon. "This was the appearance of the likeness of the glory of God" (Ezek. 1:28). Ezekiel used this term "glory of God" to express that which men can apprehend of the presence of God on earth.

During the time between the Old Testament and New Testament, Jewish rabbis used a term called "Shekinah." It comes from the Hebrew root which means "to dwell." In rabbinic literature it was a synonym for "glory" or the presence of God. The great conviction of the Old Testament is that God visited and lived with human beings.

God's presence is strengthened and enriched by his visit to earth. "And the Word was made flesh, and dwelt among us, (and we beheld his glory, the glory as of the only begotten of the Father,) full of grace and truth" (John 1:14). The life of Jesus Christ was a manifestation of glory. The word glory in the Old Testament was used repeatedly for the presence of God among people. In the desert the children of Israel "looked toward the wilderness, and, behold, the glory of the Lord appeared in the cloud" (Ex. 16:10). Before the giving of the Ten Commandments, "the glory of the Lord abode upon mount Sinai" (Ex. 24:16). When the Tabernacle had been built and equipped, "the glory of the Lord filled the tabernacle" (Ex. 40:34). When Solomon's Temple was dedicated the priests could not enter to minister "for the glory of the Lord had filled the house of the Lord" (1 Kings 8:11).

God visited time in Jesus to reveal his true character.

Jesus, the one in eternal being with God, became a temporal event at a point in time. He became a finite creature under the limitations of time. God chose to enter time and convey the real portrait of himself. Jesus revealed God's character of grace and truth. Grace is God's actions of giving people more than they deserve. Truth is God's determination to be consistent with his eternal character, predictable, and trustworthy in dealing with mankind. In the life and ministry of Jesus, there is the disclosure of grace and truth. Both belong in the picture. Grace without truth can be sentimentalism while truth without grace can be inflexible rigidity. To disclose the character of God, Jesus had a infinite tenderness with the sinner combined with an unswerving fidelity to truth.

God visited time in Jesus to rescue human beings from a predicament. The incarnation was not just a disclosure of God's character. It was also a rescue operation. "To wit, that God was in Christ, reconciling the world unto himself" (2 Cor. 5:19). Human beings rebelled against God and this estranged them from God and from others. God acted in a rescue operation to bring man to God, to fellow human beings, and to wholeness of self. All the actions of Jesus—teaching, interviews, the cross, the resurrection—tell of God's presence to reconcile erring, straying human beings.

God is still present in time. God did not retire after the resurrection. He is still a vital part of time. Jesus Christ is "the same yesterday, and to day, and for ever" (Heb. 13:8). One cannot divorce the event of God's coming to earth two thousand years ago with his presence today. The Christ who came is continually coming to us. Jesus Christ must be known as a presence here and now. Jesus confronts us now and forces us into the agnony of decision where we must choose a false existence, or Christ entering into our lives to give an authentic existence. The Spirit of God is the continuing presence of Jesus Christ. He is involved in time at this moment in his Holy Spirit.

God Stops Time

As we look at the picture of God as the timekeeper, another insight comes to us about God. We have seen that God visited time; and now we see that he will cause time to cease. Other people can tell time, but only God can tell time to stop.

The Bible speaks about an end of time. "And this gospel of the kingdom shall be preached in all the world for a witness unto all nations; and then shall the end come" (Matt. 24:14). In explaining the parable of the wheat and the tares Jesus spoke about the cessation of time. "The harvest is the end of the world" (Matt. 13:39). Jesus assured the disciples of his presence until the end: "Lo, I am with you alway, even unto the end of the world" (Matt. 28:20).

God moves time toward its goal. Seeing God as the timekeeper makes history have sense both now and later. Other views of the moving of time seem to be senseless. There is a cyclic view of history in which history is seen as repeating itself, periodically retracing its steps. The evolutionary view is one which views time progressing under its own power. In the picture of God as the timekeeper, God is seen at the beginning of time, above it yet within it and moving it towards its goal. The New Testament word used to describe God moving time toward a completion is *eschaton*.

Jesus visualized an end to history. The end would involve a final judgment, a bodily resurrection, and a final separation between the saved and lost.

The New Testament word for "end" is *telos*. It designates a termination, a cessation, a conclusion. Jesus is moving history toward the complete overcoming of all hostility to God. Time is not endless, and history will not end like a clock that runs down. Time and history are being moved to an end (*telos*) which is its goal (*eschaton*).

No one knows when God will stop time. "But of that day and that hour knoweth no man, no, not the angels which are in heaven, neither the Son, but the Father. Take ye heed, watch and pray: for ye know not when the time is" (Mark 13:32–33). Anyone attempting to set a time assumes more than God allows angels to know.

Jesus will end time to bring to completion that which is incomplete. He will perfect the imperfect. The kingdom of God has a present and future connotation. At the end of time the consummation of the present aspect of the kingdom will merge into the future, thus becoming one. The New Testament views two ages as overlapping. The Christian lives in these two orders at once, historical and the eternal. The eternal transcends time but is related to it. A further and all-important factor in the New Testament conception of time is that the end is seen to have already entered into history and become a part of it.

God will stop time completely one day. Judgment can only take place at the end of time. The full impact and meaning of an act now, good or bad, may be seen only when the full course has been run. Some sins are immediately apparent, but some are seen in their true character only when their ugly fruits are harvested. "Some men's sins are open beforehand, going before to judgment; and some men they follow after" (1 Tim. 5:24). The full effect of a lie, or lust, a sexual affair, greed, jealousy, prejudice, ill-will, malice can only be seen at the final judgment. Likewise, the full measure of good deeds is to be seen at the final judgment.

God will end time in order to bring out what people have done in relation to Christ during time. The object of the judgment is not to determine character. The omniscient Judge knows the character of every person. The purpose of the judgment is the revealing of character formed on earth during a time span. Judgment is a manifestation that which, in essence, has previously existed.

God ends time to allow people to enter into an eternal existence. God ends time to separate the people of God from those who are unwilling to be his people. All through time God is patient and long-suffering, not willing that any should perish. The New Testament offers no escape from the idea of separation from God after the closing of time for those who chose not to relate to the Lord. After time is ended, the lost person enters into an existence of a life apart from God.

When time ends, believers enter into a fuller and richer eternal existence with God. This is called heaven. Heaven is not just a time existence of day after day living. It is a life of genuine, complete, free realization of our humanity. It is the life which God willed for us by the Creator and lived by his Son, Jesus, and worked in us by his Spirit. It is an eternal life of the self-fulfillment which comes in loving and praising God; and in loving and letting ourselves be loved by other human beings.

Jesus revealed God as The Timekeeper. This picture shows us that God has no beginning, and he has no termination. He conceived the idea of time and initiated it. He became intimately involved during the process of time. Ultimately he will stop time and reign throughout eternity.

3.
The Grave Robber

Turning the pages in the picture album gives us many insights into the nature and character of God. We get some of the most interesting and helpful pictures of God when we go through the gospels and see the numerous poses. God disclosed himself to human beings in various situations that would help us see him for who he really is.

In the Gospels, an unexpected picture of God emerges. It is the picture of God as The Grave Robber. Of course, this may sound crude at first but look closer at some scenes. The first scene was in the house of Jairus. His little daughter had just died. The mourners had already started their grieving. Jesus went inside Jairus' house, took the little girl by her hand, and brought her to life again. The second scene is in a small city called Nain. A poor widow had just lost her only son in death. Jesus had compassion upon her loss. He touched the bier of the young man and told him to arise. The man was restored to life.

The third scene of Jesus' robbing a grave was in Bethany. This time death had claimed his close friend Lazarus, the brother of Martha and Mary. The death of Lazarus offered a good opportunity to disclose a fascinating feature of the nature and power of God. Jesus wanted to open the shutters and allow human beings to get one of the most powerful pictures of God. The scene was quite dramatic. Mary and Martha wept for their brother Lazarus. Jesus stood in front of the cave where Lazarus was buried. Jesus asked them to take away the stone. Martha cautioned the Master about this gesture, "Lord, by this time he stinketh: for he hath been dead four days" (John 11:39). Then the Lord told her he wanted to give an amazing picture of God for their album. "Said I not unto thee, that, if thou wouldest believe, thou shouldest see the glory of God?" (John 11:40). Then Jesus prayed. After his prayer, he called for Lazarus to come from the cave. Jesus robbed the darkness of death of another subject.

An enlargement of these three snapshots came after Jesus' personal death. From the scenes of Nain, Bethany, and Jairus' house we see that Jesus delivered others from their death. When we look at the scene of Calvary and see the time exposure of three days later, a sharper, enlarged picture emerges of God. Regarding the death of Jesus, the disciples frequently said: "God raised him up." Jesus had the power to lay down his life and the power to pick it up again. That is a picture of the grave robber!

These several scenes of victory over death furnish a picture of God as the conqueror of life's greatest enemy, namely death. Numerous people can present you with interesting methods of how to get the most out of life. But after leaving this life, there is a strange silence on how to conquer the enemy of death. Only one person gave the world a picture of how to live and how to die. The picture of God as the grave robber furnishes a portrait which the world desperately wants and needs to see.

The Life-Giver

Let's take a moment and look closer at the snapshot of Jesus raising Lazarus from the grave. The picture indicates that Lazarus, Martha, and Mary were disciples of Jesus. This would mean that Lazarus possessed real life before he died. This kind of life came as a result of Lazarus' commitment to Jesus Christ. It was a quality of life different from any other kind of life. Because of his commitment to Jesus Christ, Lazarus discovered the real meaning of life. When Lazarus died, Jesus brought him back to more days of life.

One of the most interesting facets of this portrait is that Jesus robs life of emptiness and meaninglessness. He robs the grave of the spiritually dead. The New Testament makes many statements to amplify the truth about spiritual death. The word "death" in the New Testament has several meanings. First, it can mean the physical cessation of life. Probably the word "death" was used most frequently in the bodily cessation of activity than in any other reference. Second, the word "death" can mean a spiritual state in which people may live and still be destitute of all that is worth calling "life." In this context a person can be physically alive but dead to the true meaning and purpose of life. Third, the word "death" in the New Testament can refer to the transferal from a life of selfishness or sin to a life of righteousness in Christ. Paul used this reference to describe the believer as one "dead to sin" and "alive with Christ." Finally, the term "second death" is mentioned by the writer of the Revelation (20:6,14). This term refers to the experience of the unbeliever. The unbeliever comes to physical death and finds beyond it a separation from the blessings and fellowship of God which can be described only as a "second death."

The spiritual death while one is yet alive is a real experience. Paul spoke of this experience of spiritual death: "And you . . . who were dead in trespasses and sins" (Eph. 2:1). "Even when we were dead in sins" (Eph. 2:5). "And you, being dead in your sins" (Col. 2:13). Paul taught that there is a state of moral and spiritual death even in the case of persons who are otherwise intensely alive. It is quite possible for one to manifest the most vigorous physical and mental life, while at the same time being spiritually dead. To be spiritually alive means a consciousness of divine realities. It means to be conscious of our inner world of feelings, attitudes, intentions, values, and principles; as well as consciousness of God and our relationship with other people and with the material world. Only Jesus can deliver one from the spiritual state of death.

Not only does the Bible teach that a life chosen apart from God means spiritual death, but experience and observation teaches this reality. Science and technological advances have sought to rescue human beings from the deadness of living. They have made life more comfortable. But technology cannot bring meaning. It only brings comfort. Sociology has worked frantically to bring meaningful relationships with other people. The discord among human beings has sounded the alarm for someone to give the world something to enable us to live together. Psychological studies of the mind of a person has been intensified in the last fifty years in an effort to seek to give man an understanding of himself and how to have a more meaningful life.

The question arises, "Who will rescue the human race from this spiritual death?" The answer is obvious when we look at God's portrait in the gospels. Everywhere you find Jesus as a life-giver. He delivers human beings from a meaningless existence to a life of meaning. Jesus Christ is the only one who can reach into the pitiful condition which man has placed himself and give him a meaningful life. In one sense of the word we can say that Jesus robs the grave of spiritual death and brings the subject to new life.

Jesus brings life to the believer. Just as there is more than one kind of death, so there is more than one kind of resurrection from the dead. In the New Testament the word "resurrection" can mean the physical restoration of a person to life. It is also used to represent the spiritual operation of God's power in the experience of every person. To Martha and Mary, Jesus said: "I am the resurrection, and the life: he that believeth in me, though he were dead, yet shall he live" (John 11:25).

The authentic Christian experience is a resurrection from spiritual death to spiritual life. This means that Jesus raises people from badness to goodness. Jesus raises morally upright people who want and need a new kind of life. The authentic Christian experience is a spiritual resurrection.

Living can be a form of dying. The Genesis story of Adam and Eve in their sin and punishment is a good illustration. God had warned them they would die if they sinned. When they rebelled against God, they experienced shame and hid from God. They began to degenerate in character. This is the real death—separation from God, divine judgment, degeneration in character, and conflict in relation to others.

Jesus robs the spiritual grave of people. He makes life rich and full. Jesus gives a person the ability to realize who he is, to actualize his potential. Consequently, deep satisfaction results. Because he is becoming the person he yearns to be, he can build loving and trusting relations with others. Jesus is a life-giver. He gives a new quality of life when one opens his life in faith. This will not prevent physical death. However, death will not destroy this kind of life. It will continue with the Lord.

What an amazing disclosure from the portrait of God. He is the life-giver. He gives a quality of life which is fulfilling and deeply satisfying.

The Death Destroyer

Let's look at the picture and see another facet of God. Mary and Martha demonstrated great grief and disappointment over the death of their brother. Martha even expressed anger over Jesus not being present to heal Lazarus of his great sickness. "Lord, if thou hadst been here, my brother had not died" (John 11:21). There was a note of doom and defeat in Martha's voice and on her face. Death to her was life's greatest enemy, and it had claimed her brother.

Jesus used this occasion to paint the truth that God

destroyed death. The three snapshots where Jesus restored a dead body to life furnishes a microcosm of how Jesus Christ would defeat death by his death. Soon after Jesus raised Lazarus from the grave, he faced his own death. What would be the results of his death? Would his departure from life be as the others? Or would he actually die and be raised by God as he predicted? The New Testament contains numerous snapshots of the resurrected Christ. To be exact, there are eleven scenes of the appearances of Jesus during the forty days between his death and his ascension.

Jesus conquered death. One of the greatest disclosures of God is that he conquered death. Jesus lived and ministered in the world. The enemy of death constantly stared him in the face. It was his worst enemy. Death definitely did its worst on Calvary. Brutal death at its most decisive and overwhelming worst seemed to triumph that day on Calvary. Death seemed to have claimed its prey as Jesus died on that fateful Friday.

But death had a short-lived triumph. Death tenaciously held the Son of God like an iron wire. Something happened. God raised him up. The pangs of death were loosened. Death could not hold its prey. Something tragic happened to the Son of God that day on Calvary. But something happened to death itself.

Numerous New Testament writers affirm the reality that Jesus did something to conquer death. Rather arrogantly, Paul said: "O death, where is thy sting? O grave, where is thy victory? The sting of death is sin and the strength of sin is the law. But thanks be to God, which giveth us the victory through our Lord Jesus Christ" (1 Cor. 15:55–57). These questions have the tone of one who jeers at conquered enemies.

In one of Eugene O'Neill's plays, *Lazarus Laughed,* the truth that Jesus conquered death is dramatized. O'Neill tells how the brother of Mary and Martha, who was raised from the dead by Jesus, left the old home in Bethany and traveled and settled in Greece. On one occasion at the square in Athens he met the almost insane and utterly cruel Gaius Caligula, who had been chosen by the Emperor Tiberius as his successor. Once some spies informed Caligula that the people hated him. Caligula responded, "Let them hate—so long as they fear us! We must keep death dangling before their eyes . . . I like to watch men die." Lazarus confronted Caligula, and the mad ruler accused Lazarus of teaching people to laugh at death. He threatened Lazarus with execution. But Lazarus looked into his face and laughed, and answered: "Death is dead, Caligula. Death is dead."

Jesus robs death of its many fears. This is not to say that Jesus allows a believer to face death passively. No, everyone has either conscious or unconscious fears about death. All of us have numerous horrors about dying. We dread the pain associated with dying. We also dread the fact of oblivion. Humanly speaking, we have a tendency to think that death will end our personal existence. Maybe our life is so tied to the physical body that we think that when it dies that's all there is. Then we fear separation from our family, our friends, our associates. Death causes us to fear because it is a great unknown. We have a tendency to want all the answers; to fear guesses; to long for certainties. Faith does not seem as sure as visual knowledge.

What a picture we get of how much God identified with human beings as we look at Jesus facing his death! Jesus went through the human struggles before his hour of death. As he wrestled with death's certainty in Gethsemane, one can get a glimpse of the human qualities of the Son of God.

Jesus has taught us how to face death and rob it of its haunting fears. First, Jesus walked toward his death. He did not try to evade the fact of his death. Human beings try by numerous means to repress the reality of death. Jesus did not walk away from death trying to suppress it. He walked toward death, and he gives the strength for any disciple to walk toward their death. H. C. Brown, Jr., professor of preaching for many years at Southwestern Baptist Theological Seminary, struggled to gain victory over a congenital heart disease. Brown stated that a friend helped him develop a philosophy for facing death: "The way to defeat your fear is to walk toward it." Jesus can give the courage to face death honestly and openly.

Second, Jesus wants us to realize the kind of life we have. Jesus faced his death with the assurance that the Father would give him a greater life. It was the kind of life that could not be destroyed. The Christian has been given a life by God which cannot be ended by the experience of death. Eternal life is a present reality which not even death is able to remove. What God gives to a Christian, he intends to preserve.

Third, Jesus faced death with the assurance of God's presence. Jesus trusted God all the way through death's experience. Because Jesus trusted the Lord, he recognized the presence of God all the way through the experience of dying. Jesus gives the assurance that death does not remove his presence. He will be with us.

Jesus robs death of its victory and of its horror. The picture needs to be distributed to a dying world.

The Transition Maker

You haven't seen all the picture yet. There is more in the picture of the grave robber than any commentator on the picture can tell. The snapshot of Jesus at the graveside of Lazarus gives us another insight into the power of God. Jesus said to Martha, "I am the resurrection, and the life: he that believeth in me, though he were dead, yet shall he live: And whosoever liveth and believeth in me shall never die" (John 11:25–26). Jesus said to believe in him meant to appropriate in advance the fulfillment awaited in the future.

The portrait of God with Lazarus' death and resurrection as a background presents an interesting facet of God's character. We have seen that Jesus robs spiritual death and gives eternal life on this earth. Furthermore, we have seen in the picture that Jesus defeats the enemy of death. He gives a resurrection beyond the grave. He causes a transition. Death then to a believer is a means of moving from one aspect of enjoying life to another aspect of enjoying life.

Jesus makes a transition from one kind of body to another kind of body. Raymond Moody, a psychiatrist, tells interesting testimonies of people who have been pronounced clinically dead. In his book *Life After Life*, he relates numerous experiences of people who returned from the experience of death. His works are interesting, but in each case the person returned to life with a physical body. Jesus gives a new body. The Greek word *anastasis* means to raise up the body from the clutches of death. Any view of future survival which leaves out a body cannot be spoken of as a resurrection in the New Testament sense of the term. Actually the raising of Lazarus was more of a resuscitation to physical life. It was a demonstration that Jesus has power to effect a transition. The resurrection of a person is far more than resuscitation. It means a miraculous giving of another body.

Let's look at the resurrection of Jesus after his death. The New Testament presents the resurrection of Jesus as a fact. There is no attempt to prove it; it is stated as a fact. Looking at the snapshots of Jesus' resurrected body might help us understand how Jesus gives a new body to believers. Jesus' body was a tangible one. Many people saw Jesus after his resurrection. Several people talked with him. Some even touched him. This would seem to indicate that the resurrection of Jesus was not a hallucination.

The body of Jesus was a transcendent body. The body of Lazarus was resuscitated. It was restored to the natural plane of life. Yet, Jesus' body was not subject to space, material objects, or time. He appeared in a room where doors and windows were closed. He vanished from two disciples on the road to Emmaus. The body of Jesus transcended the ordinary operation of laws in the material and natural level of life. God had given Jesus a body adapted to the needs of the world. His resurrection body was adapted to the needs on a high level of living.

What a cherished picture of God! This means that God has given human beings a body to enjoy this world. It is adapted to the needs of earth. Death marks a transition. After death, God gives believers a body suited to the life in glory. Paul made some excellent comments on the truth in 1 Corinthians 15:44–49. He described the Christian's transition, "It is sown a natural body; it is raised a spiritual body" (1 Cor. 15:44). The physical body will not die and be raised a spirit. It is planted a natural body, and it is raised a spiritual body. The earthly body has been especially suited to the needs of life in the physical. The new body will be adapted to the needs of the spiritual life.

Jesus robs the experience beyond the grave of emptiness and oblivion. In Shakespeare's play *Hamlet* there is a struggle of death and existence. Hamlet contemplates, "To be or not to be?" This has been the struggle of many. Does death terminate me as a person? When my physical body dies, is that all of me? No, Jesus paints the picture that death is a transition from a rich to a richer life.

The richer life is one of peacefulness and rest. Jesus gives a peaceful life now, but after death there is a drastic transition. Conflict, strife, and suffering hinder this peacefulness now. After death there will be a life of joyous praise, active thanksgiving and glad worship. Death does not finalize our goals and potentials. Jesus allows us to actualize our true selves and to reach our fullest potential. Jesus robs the future of oblivion, of the unknown, of separation, and of unfulfillment.

4.
The Coin Collector

One of my boys handed me a book to show me an unusual picture. It was an ink sketch of a cabin near a beautiful river with a background of dense woods. Under the picture there was an instruction to find ten different objects in the picture. It read: "What else do you see in the picture?" My eye could not see any other objects. I had to take some time to look intensely for other objects. I observed the picture closely, and several other pictures became evident. After I saw the hidden objects, I wondered why I did not see them at first glance. They became so obvious.

Perhaps the stories of the seeking shepherd and the loving father are the only two pictures a person sees when he looks the first time at Luke 15. But the more you look at the chapter the more another picture emerges. It is the picture of a woman seeking for a lost coin. Like the two other parables the picture of the lost coin gives us amazing insights into God's feelings and actions. Let us look closer into this story and see some great glimpses of God.

Jesus drew beautiful pictures of God through the use of simple stories. A humble woman lost a silver coin in some dark spot of her windowless room. The silver could have been part of a necklace. It could have been her Temple tax. It could have been a drachma or the earnings for one day. As quickly as the woman missed the coin, she lighted a lamp and with a crude broom swept every corner, till at last the tinkle of the coin signaled the end of her search. So she called her friends and neighbors and said, "Let's have a celebration, for I have found that precious coin of mine!"

Jesus spoke this parable to a group of people who had the wrong picture of God. They thought that God only cared for certain groups, namely scribes and Pharisees. Knowing that these religious groups had made a caricature of God as exerting an exclusive love, Jesus told a simple story about this woman who searched for a coin. It made the point simple enough that anyone losing a coin would search diligently for it. In the same manner God searches for anyone who gets lost from his fellowship. The story yields the portrait of God as the great Coin Collector.

Collecting coins is a favorite pursuit of many people today. You can see people walking down beaches and over the countryside searching for rare coins. I have a friend who has a vending machine business. He spends every Saturday morning searching through the week's receipts for rare coins. The formal term for coin collecting is numismatics. It began in the fifteenth and sixteenth centuries with the Italian Renaissance. At that time there was a search for Greco-Roman coins. Coins are valuable for a number of reasons. Their value is often determined by their age. Finding an old coin means that you have something unique. Also, the value of a coin is often determined by the mint marks. The maker of the coin often determines a coin's value. People collect coins because of the preciousness and value of them.

God is The Coin Collector. He searches for life's dearest treasure, a human being. Humanity has the image of God. Within every human being is the breath of life. Look closely at the picture of the woman searching for a coin and it will disclose many traits about God as the coin collector.

The Preciousness of People

The coin mentioned in the story was a drachma, a silver

coin worth about sixteen cents in American money. The coin could have been a part of several things. It could have been a part of the slender resources of that household. At the time of Jesus a working man's daily wage was equivalent to sixteen cents, a drachma. Most of the people lived from day to day, and little stood between them and real hunger. The woman could have searched for the lost drachma out of necessity. It was important to recover the coin to get the family something to eat.

Alfred Plummer in his work on Luke in the *International Critical Commentary* contends that the coin could have related to a Jewish marriage custom. Many Jewish girls saved until they had ten pieces of silver which they strung together and wore as a necklace or a headdress. It was her property and remained absolutely so. It could not be taken, even for a debt. It was the nearest ancient equivalent to a marriage ring. The woman could have searched for the coin out of deep sentiment.[1]

Regardless of the exact meaning of the coin, one thing is certain. The coin was precious to her. If it were part of her savings, the coin needed to be found to feed her family. If the coin were part of a wedding symbol, it was needed for the sake of sentiment. The point is abundantly clear—the coin was a precious possession to the woman. Likewise, human beings are precious to the Lord. Jesus gave the religious leaders a portrait of God who regards everyone as precious.

Human beings are precious because they are the crown of God's creation. Every person is dear to God, for God's breath resides in them. Human beings are the most unique and most valuable part of God's creation. W. T. Conner summarized human nature into four qualities: Intelligence, or the power to think rationally about oneself or God; Rational Affection, or the ability to move toward goodness as a goal; Free Will, or the power to determine the direction of one's life; Moral Nature, an innate sense of right and wrong.[2]

These are the unique qualities of a human being. God made human beings with these unusual and unique qualities. No other part or element of creation has the capacities of a human being. Something precious to God is at stake when a human being is lost.

Human beings are important because of their potential. A woman searched for a coin because of its potential either for food or for a symbol of her marriage. Human beings are precious because God made them with so much potential. God made man in order that he might serve God and in order to have dominion over all the created order. One fulfills God's intents as he is properly related to nature, to others, and supremely to God. No other part of creation can have dominion over nature. No other element of creation can do justice, love mercy, and walk humbly with God.

Human beings have rebelled stubbornly against God's high intentions. Instead of the wonderful communion between God and man, sin has brought guilt as a barrier to man's approach to God. This guilt causes man to picture God as the enemy. Jesus wanted to correct this erroneous picture of God. He drew a picture of God continuing to track and to recover rebellious human beings. The coin collector looks for precious people with the desire to restore them to their useful and intended potential.

Human beings are valuable or precious because of God's assessment of value. The woman placed value on the coin. God places a value on the human soul. There is no price equal to the worth of a soul. One human being is worth more than all of the created order. Jesus asked, "For what is a man profited, if he shall gain the whole world, and lose his own soul? or what shall a man give in exchange for his soul?" (Matt. 16:26).

A friend gave me a pamphlet on ginseng, a plant that grows wild in the mountains. It is valuable for its roots. Chinese and other Orientals claim that the ginseng plant has great medical qualities. They brew it into a tea and take it for numerous medical reasons. Ginseng is an expensive herb. There is no understanding of the value of ginseng without a knowledge of its use. You cannot know the value of a person until you see his preciousness and usefulness in the sight of God.

An Intense Search

When the woman discovered that she had lost the coin, she began an intensive search. Notice her actions. She lit a candle. Her little house had been built without windows to keep out the hot, Eastern sun. This also inevitably kept out the daylight also. So the woman took a lamp, such as it was. It was a wick floating in a saucer of clay filled with oil. She swept and looked diligently for that coin.

Jesus was a master at portraying a facet of the nature and character of God. The persistent, diligent search of the woman coin collector gives an excellent insight on God's search for lost people. Any coin collector would be involved in a search. The search of the woman gives an interesting insight into the work which God does for lost human beings. Because he considers their value, he searches diligently for them.

Jesus said, "No man can come to me, except the Father which hath sent me draw him" (John 6:44). No person can claim the credit for repentance or faith. If a person repents of his sins and expresses faith in Christ, he does so because God has been seeking that person. Man does not move to God, but God moves to man.

The focus in the picture of the coin collector is clear. Jesus asked, "What woman would not search for a lost coin?" Any woman would search for a lost coin which was valuable. God is like that. He initiates the search for lost human beings. The entire picture album (the Bible) contains pictures of God taking the initiative to initiate recovery for lost yet precious human beings. In both the Old Testament and the New Testament we get the clear picture of God searching, for searching love is intimately a part of God's nature.

To have a picture either of man searching for God or a God who refuses to search for man is an overexposure. You have allowed too much humanity into your picture.

God seeks with a purpose in mind. The woman sought for the lost coin, for she had a purpose for it. Either she would spend it for food, use it as a Temple tax, or put it back into her headdress. Coin collecting was not a hobby to her. The coin had real value for her.

Jesus has a purpose in seeking lost people. When a person becomes a Christian, he is not brought into relationship with God as a matter of chance; he is saved in pursuance of an eternal purpose of God. God works diligently to bring us to himself. He wants to restore us.

What is the purpose that God has in searching for us? It is not for sport. It has a real significance. God intends to bring us to himself. God wants man to have a positive relationship with him. Man's stubborn rebellion has impaired man's relationship with God. God wants to restore that relationship. This is why God seeks man. But God also wants us to fulfill a happy relationship with others. Man's lostness deprived him of a healthy social atmosphere. God wants to restore relations of an individual with another individual; of an individual with society; and an individual with his culture. God is not pleased with man's injustices to his fellowman, so he greatly desires to restore man to his fellowman.

Man's "awayness" from God has caused a duplicity within himself. Man has been marred by the departure. God intends to recover man in order to bring wholeness to the individual. That's why God searches. He wants you with him. He wants you to be able to relate to others. He wants you at your best self.

God seeks sacrificially. One word in Jesus' story of the coin collector speaks volumes about God's nature. It is the word "till" in Luke 15:8. It describes the persistent pursuit of God. God is willing to go to any length to bring man back to him. The search God made for sinners cost him an enormous price. It sent him to Calvary.

Looking at what God did to bring humanity back brings a beautiful picture of God. By Christ's work and devotion, reconciliation was wrought between God and man.

Why did Jesus have to sacrifice himself to recover man from lostness? Why couldn't God just say, "I forgive you," and let it go at that? Suppose I do something that deeply hurts my wife, and she says to me, "That's all right. It doesn't make any difference. Forget it." What this says is that she does not care enough about me to be touched by anything I say or do. Actually this action says, "You are not important to me." Real love means caring enough to be hurt. It means to care enough to put oneself in the other's shoes, and sharing his guilt as if it were ones own. Real love costs.

God loves mankind too much to dismiss his lostness with a casual, "It doesn't matter." Action proved that his love and forgiveness was genuine. God wants to stand with us and share the loneliness and alienation of our lostness. He suffers that loneliness, alienation, and guilt. The divine coin collector makes an intensive search. He still searches for lost people.

The Joy of God

The story of the coin collector concluded with a picture of joy. After the woman found the lost coin, she called her friends and neighbors together: "Let's have a celebration," she said, "for I have found that precious coin of mine." She was filled with uncontrollable joy when she gained the coin that she had lost.

The Pharisees had a picture of a God who takes delight in the perishing of sinners. They had a saying, "There is joy before God when those who provoke him perish from the world." [3] But Jesus gave the real picture of God. Only Jesus could describe heaven. Only Jesus would dare to say that God and his angels are like that woman and her neighbors. "Likewise, I say unto you, there is joy in the presence of the angels of God over one sinner that repenteth" (Luke 15:10).

In all three parables recorded in Luke 15, the good shepherd, the coin collector, and the loving father—there is a note of joy. When the shepherd found the lost sheep, he called his friends and neighbors for a time of rejoicing. The woman did the same thing. When the young boy returned from the far country, there was excitement in the father's requests to the servants. He called for a joyous celebration.

This picture portrays an amazing picture of God as joyous. If you could see a picture of God, would you conceive him with a smile? Sometimes our ideas of God become so stilted and barren that we think of God as impassive. Instead of life photographs of God we have a tendency to think of God in impersonal, academic flash cards. We sometimes have a tendency to think that the mood of his being is neither torn by rebellion nor gratified by commitment. But Jesus spoke of God as one who rejoices.

Most books on theology have little to say about the joy of God. You can find much about the holiness, righteousness, omnipotence, omnipresence, invincibility, unchangeable attributes of God. The picture of God that Jesus gives is a living, personal God. God acts, speaks, knows, wills, decides. He loves, regrets, and rejoices. He can be angry, compassionate, jealous, merciful. God is not something displayed by theological flash cards. He is a person revealed supremely in Jesus Christ and recorded in the gospels.

"Rejoicing!" That gives us the picture of God without the frowning, judgmental face. In the picture we can see eyes wet not with reproach but with happiness. God made human beings to enjoy. He knows how to rejoice and to enjoy his creation. The hardworking woman was thrilled to see the missing coin again. Imagine God's excitement if some person repents and commits his life to the Lord to walk with the Lord. When you get a picture of God from the gospels, you shall see him as Jesus portrays him, not with a frown but with a smile.

Notice what brings God joy. Find out the actions that bring a person joy and you will discover the character of a person. The shepherd found the sheep. The woman found the coin. A wandering boy was lost but was found. The word "found" describes the reason God is joyous. Nothing brings delight to God any more than the restoration of character to an individual.

A poor outcast woman died in a hospital in Cincinnati. Among her personal effects were six stanzas of a poem entitled "Beautiful Snow." We do not know the author.

> Once I was pure as the snow, but I fell,
> Fell like the snow—but from heaven to hell;
> Fell to be trampled as filth of the street,
> Fell to be scoffed, to be spit on and beat;
> Pleading—cursing—dreading to die,
>
> Selling my soul to whoever would buy;
> Dealing in shame for a morsel of bread;
> Hating the living, and fearing the dead.
> Merciful God! have I fallen so low?
> And yet I was once like the beautiful snow.
>
> Once I was fair as the beautiful snow,
> With an eye like a crystal, a heart like its glow;
> Once I was loved for my innocent grace,
> Flattered and sought for the charms of my face!
> Father—mother—sisters,—all,

God and myself, I have lost by my fall;
The veriest wretch that goes shivering by
Will make a wide sweep lest I wander too nigh;
For all that is on or about me, I know,
There is nothing that's pure as the beautiful snow.

Helpless and foul as the trampled snow,
Sinner, despair not! Christ stoopeth low
To rescue the soul that is lost in sin,
And raise it to life and enjoyment again.
    Groaning—bleeding—dying for thee,

The Crucified hung on the cursed tree!
His accents of pity fall soft on thine ear.
Is there mercy for me? Will he heed my weak prayer?
O God! in the stream that for sinners did flow,
Wash me, and I shall be whiter than snow! [3]

Nothing brings more joy to God than a lost person who comes home again. In Jesus' picture of God, joy is one of the dominant colorings of God. When character is gained, God rejoices.

5.
The Miracle Worker

William Gibson has written one of the most beautiful dramas of our time. It is entitled *The Miracle Worker*. His play relates the inspiring story of Helen Keller. It was first a success on Broadway and then an Academy Award-winning motion picture. Soon after the little girl had been born into the home of an Alabama couple, she seemed consigned to a living death. A raging fever left Helen Keller unable to see, hear, or speak. Surrounded by darkness and silence, she became akin to a wild animal tolerated by benevolent, but puzzled, parents.

Anne Sullivan came into the blighted life of Helen Keller. She was contracted to be her teacher. She desperately wanted to reach into the little girl's life and open a channel of communication with the outside world of reality. Since Helen had been denied the normal gifts of sight and sound, Miss Sullivan worked with her remaining sense of touch. She sought to establish contact with the buried hopes and expressions of Helen Keller. Patiently Miss Sullivan traced the letters of the blind alphabet and guided young Helen's hand to touch objects for which the letters stood. Slowly but surely insight dawned upon Miss Keller's mind. The bridge between symbol and reality had been crossed. She began to perceive and to communicate with the world around her. As a result of Anne Sullivan's creative and persistent teaching, Helen Keller became one of the most luminous lives of the twentieth century.

William Gibson called Anne Sullivan "The Miracle Worker." She deserved that title. Nothing less than a miracle could have brought light and life where there had been only darkness and death. The transformation of Helen Keller was incredible. Miss Sullivan's touch upon Helen Keller's life will remain a great inspiration for those who read or see the story.

One of the great portraits of God in the gospels could be labeled "The Miracle Worker." Reading the Gospels we see numerous poses where God reached into lives of darkness and despair and brought life and light. The miracles of Jesus Christ disclose the powerful influence of the Lord upon nature and upon the lives of human beings. Jesus demonstrated numerous traits of God in the miracles: God's compassion over needy human beings; God's desire to help people; God's will for people's wholeness, not sickness; and God's power over disease, birth defects, and demon possession.

Jesus portrayed many wonderful truths about God in the healing of the paralyzed man recorded in Mark 2:1–12. The story is interesting. Four men brought a paralyzed man to see and hear the Master. The large crowds prohibited the men from getting the paralyzed man to Jesus. Nonetheless, the men were determined to get the man to Jesus. They lowered him through the roof, and Jesus worked a miracle in the man's life. The miracle discloses many aspects about the character of God.

God Values Personhood

The first word Jesus spoke to the paralyzed man was, "Son." On the surface that might seem to be a courteous greeting. But the Greek New Testament records the word Jesus used. It was *teknon*. This word was one which reflected that Jesus acknowledged with tenderness the personhood of the paralyzed man. Jesus knew that the paralyzed, the diseased, and the sick were looked upon as property and not primarily as persons. They were regarded as something less than human. Within the mind of the paralyzed man, he felt a low sense of worth. When Jesus said, "Son," it was miraculous. Jesus actually said to him, "Irrespective of what others may think of you or what you think of yourself, you are somebody." Think of God saying that to everyone. "Son, you are somebody."

God looks upon every person with a great sense of value. Many looked upon the paralyzed man, and they disregarded him. They considered him as something that littered the landscape. To many he was a nuisance with his outstretched hand wanting a piece of bread or a coin. But Jesus looked upon the man with a different view. He considered the paralyzed and even other outcasts as persons of immense worth and value.

God has an immense estimate upon every person who lives. No one needs to consider themselves as a nobody. Oftentimes we are affected by the feelings of society about human beings instead of God's estimate. Society judges a person's worth with such factors as the ethnic group to which they belong, the section of town they live in, the possessions they have, the achievements they have made, and numerous other superficial standards.

Jesus went about disclosing God's estimate and feelings toward people. Jesus made the sick and the handicapped feel important. He lifted men's attitude toward womanhood. He valued children. He saw a new potential from those beset with a bad moral record. He taught the affluent that life does not consist of possessions. Beneath many episodes in the ministry of the Master could be written, "Friend, God places a high value upon you."

Paul Tournier in *A Doctor's Casebook in the Light of the Bible* writes of a patient who was the youngest daughter of a large family, a family which the father found it very difficult to support. One day the child heard her father mutter despairingly, referring to her: "We could have done without that one!" [1] What a tragedy to think that way about a daughter! Yet many people living in our world think that we could do well without some people. God never has that attitude toward anyone.

The story of Muretus enshrines a great truth. Muretus was a wandering scholar, very learned and very poor. In his wanderings he fell ill and was taken to the place where the destitute were kept. They did not know that he was a scholar and that he understood the scholar's Latin. The doctors discussed his case in Latin. They were saying that he was a poor creature of value to no one, and it was unnecessary to expend care and money on such a worthless one. Muretus looked up and answered in their own Latin, "Call no man worthless for whom Christ died!"

God seeks to make everyone look at themselves as a person of value. By using such a greeting as "Son," Jesus communicated the fact that he accepted the paralyzed man as a person. But the man needed to respect and to regard himself as a person. Whenever a person discovers the fact that God loves and cares for him, he will discover the Master with a proper respect for himself.

Nowhere does the Bible have a portrait of a God who wants a person to look consistently down upon themselves. Understanding the way God feels about us enhances the way we must feel about ourselves. Seeing our sinful condition and examining our inner being might cause us to think that God looks down on us. We know that we look down on ourselves. No, the Bible gives us a marvelous picture of God. It shows us a God who loves and values us irrespective of who we may be. If God values us with such immense worth, we ought to take a closer look at ourselves. It will result in seeing a person, the crown of God's creation who has rebelled. The rebellion does not destroy God's value of us. Neither should our rebellion destroy the fact that we are persons of importance and immense capabilities.

I once heard the story of two boys who went to their minister, requesting some type of project to help people. The pastor thought a moment and then told them to read the Bible to a blind man each week. They went to the blind man's house and told him of their plans. He was delighted. "At what place in the Bible do you want us to begin reading?" "Well, since you are going to be here each week," the blind man said, "let's read through the New Testament and start with Matthew." The boys started their reading with the first chapter and the first verse. They started reading the "begets." "Let's skip all these names, sir," they requested of the old man. "No, keep reading," he said. The boys read with effort through the "begets" of Matthew. Then they noticed tears going down the blind man's cheeks. "What is so emotional about a list of names?" they asked. The blind man replied, "God knowed everyone of those fellars, and he knew them by name. Boys, that makes me feel important to know that God knows me and he knows my name."

God Pardons People

Jesus spoke another word to the paralyzed man. He said, "Thy sins be forgiven thee" (Mark 2:5). This was another disclosure of a trait of God. Jesus' word shares the truth that God wants to pardon sinners not to condemn them. Mysteriously, some caricatures of God have emerged through the years that God is angry with human beings and is intending to "get them." Throw away that concept. You didn't get it from the Bible. Look at this scene where God acted in Jesus Christ to forgive a paralyzed, sinful man.

God laments over our guilt. The paralyzed man had a terrible guilt complex. He lived in an environment where the Jews integrally connected sin and suffering. Most people said that if a person was suffering he must have sinned. That is in fact the argument that Job's friends produced. Eliphaz the Temanite said, "Remember, I pray thee, who ever perished, being inocent? or where were the righteous cut off?" (Job 4:7). The rabbis had a saying, "There is no sick man healed of his sickness until all his sins have been forgiven him." Therefore, the paralyzed man lived amid people who thought that God was angry with him. Of course all suffering may be attributed to sin in a general way, but we would not attribute specific incidents of illness to sin.

Jesus did not try to settle the complicated question of the intricate relationship of sin and suffering. God is not interested in furnishing us with theological answers. Instead, he seeks to furnish us with an adequacy in our troubles. It would not have helped the paralyzed man to know why he was paralyzed. He needed help with his troubled conscience.

God laments over our troubled conscience which is disturbed because of our sin. Psychologists quote a case of a girl who played the piano in the cinema in the days of the silent films. Normally she performed well, but immediately when the lights went out and cigarette smoke filled the auditorium, she was paralyzed. Examination revealed no physical cause whatever. Under hypnosis it was discovered that when she was very young, only a few weeks old, she had been lying in an elaborate cot arched with lace. Her mother leaned over her smoking a cigarette. The draperies caught fire. They were extinguished immediately and no physical harm was done to the girl. But her subconscious mind remembered this terror. The smell of smoke in the cinema acted on the unconscious mind and paralyzed her body.[2] The paralyzed man had a deep consciousness of guilt.

Guilt plagues human beings. God is deeply concerned about all types of guilt. James A. Knight in the book *Conscience and Guilt* speaks about three kinds of guilt. First, there is a real guilt caused by a deliberate, willful disobedience toward God and other persons. The guilt arises from disobedience. Second, there is an imposed guilt. This is a result of one's projected feelings. People establish human ideals or values, and they feel "guilty" when they do not live up to these ideals. Third, there is an existential guilt. This is a guilt which arises because we are part of the human situation.[3] For example, most Americans did not violate any rules against Southeast Asia, but we feel "guilty" about the war.

God wants to forgive and to alleviate our guilt. You will notice that Jesus gave the paralyzed man a pardon before he healed him of his paralysis. This shows that God is deeply concerned about sin at the deepest level of our lives. For the Lord to forgive the man would have removed the man's morbid guilty conscience. That is a great portrait of God—a forgiving God. He says, "Child, do not let your sins disturb you. I will forgive!"

The crowd was shocked to hear Jesus' statement, "Thy sins be forgiven thee!" The Jews taught that only God could forgive sin. Jesus dramatically displayed the heart and holiness of God. God is not mad—wanting to act in stern, severe, austere justice. God revealed himself in the life and ministry of Jesus to have a heart yearning with love and eager to forgive.

The paralyzed man got a beautiful portrait of God the day he was healed. That day he discovered that God was not as he had thought him to be. Jesus taught him that God loved him and wanted to forgive him. Maybe the reason people characterize God as a stern exacting God is because they are amazed since he forgives us. Once I read a statement of Paul Tillich which said: "The hardest thing for me to accept is the fact that God has forgiven and accepted me."

God Empowers for New Possibilities

The third word Jesus spoke to the man suggests another marvelous trait of God. Jesus said, "Arise, and take up thy bed, and go thy way into thine house" (Mark 2:11). These words reveal that God empowers people for a new possibility. Four men could get the man into the house. But only God himself could cause the man to walk out of the house. This gives us a portrait of the powerful God who is capable of giving a new possibility for life.

God changes life-styles. Think about the life-style of the paralyzed man. For years he had been confined to a pallet. Moving from place to place required benevolent care from others. He requested that people put him in a place conducive to begging. Perhaps he asked the four men to take him to hear and see the great teacher, Jesus of Nazareth. Being confined to a pallet and being unable to move about freely led to a monotonous and depressing way of life.

Jesus changed this man's way of living when he told him to take up his pallet. The man got up off the pallet slowly. The crowd rejoiced. The man praised the Master for his marvelous power. Yet, there was more to his new life than shouting and praising. Jesus wanted him to take up the bed and go to the house. This could have been a command to take up domestic responsibilities. Irrespective of the implications of the Lord's command, the insight of the Lord's power to change life-styles is evident. Because of the power of God displayed in Jesus, the man walked away with his pallet to go to a new way of living. He left the practice of begging to accept an occupation of usefulness to the community and to his family.

As one looks through the Gospel narratives, the portrait of God as a life-changing power comes into sharp focus. This trust is revealed throughout history. Human beings can have their lives changed by the tremendous power of God. In our day an example of a changed life is Malcolm Muggeridge. For years Muggeridge used his pen in Great Britain to attack the Christian faith, the Christian ethic, and the Christian church. He experienced a transforming conversion. After his conversion he wrote *Jesus Rediscovered,* which represents a means of sharing his life-changing experience with Jesus.

God directs in new activities. Jesus told the man to get up off the pallet and to go home to his family. Maybe we see something in the portrait that is not completely evident, but I think I see God as one who directs life to new activities. That is, he is not just a tremendous transactor. He is not one who merely forgives us of sins and gives power to walk, but he also directs us into meaningful activities.

God directs those in whom he works his miraculous change to serve the needs of humanity. Jesus dramatized the trait of God's ambition to be one who desires service to human needs. God works miracles in our lives that we might be "miracle workers" to the lives of other people. Jesus directed the paralyzed man who had been healed to be a blessing to the lives of other people. Others can see God when we serve them in the name of Jesus. The world got a great picture of God when Jesus came to serve. Today's world can get a picture of God when people serve the needs of others in the name of Jesus Christ.

Look at the miracles of the Master. What a tremendous glimpse of God they give us. Poetry has given us one of the greatest commentaries of God's portrait as The Miracle Worker.

The Touch of the Master's Hand

'Twas battered and scarred, and the auctioneer
   Thought it scarcely worth his while
To waste much time on the old violin,
   But he held it up with a smile;
"What am I bidden, good folks," he cried,
   "Who'll start the bidding for me?
A dollar—one dollar—then two, only two—
   Two dollars, and who'll make it three?
Going for three,"—but no—

From the room far back, a grayhaired man
Came forward and picked up the bow;
  Then wiping the dust from the old violin,
And tightening the loosened strings,
  He played a melody pure and sweet
As a caroling angel sings.

The music ceased and the auctioneer,
  With a voice that was quiet and low,
Said, "Now what am I bid for the old violin?"
  And he held it up with the bow;
"A thousand dollars—and who'll make it two?
  Two thousand and who'll make it three?
Three thousand once—three thousand twice—
  And going—and gone," cried he;
The people cheered, but some of them cried,
  "We don't understand;
What changed its worth?" Quick came the reply,
  "The touch of a master's hand."

And many a man with life out of tune,
  And battered and scarred with sin,
Is auctioned cheap to a thoughtless crowd,
  Much like the old violin,
A mess of pottage—a glass of wine,
  A game—and he travels on;
He's going once—and going twice—
  He's going—and almost gone!
But the Master comes, and the foolish crowd,
  Never can quite understand.
The worth of a soul, and the change that's wrought
  By the touch of the Master's hand.[4]

6.
The Waiting Father

All of us have our favorite family pictures. During my courtship and married life, I have accumulated numerous pictures of my wife. My favorite pose of her is a portrait which hangs in our living room. The portrait shows her standing beside a chair which was our first piece of furniture. She is wearing a dress that I gave her for an anniversary gift. In the background of the portrait, there is a flower arrangement she made and a picture of her parents. The portrait is so lifelike that one expects her to speak.

Since the birth of our two sons, the cameras have been busy. The bulbs flashed through nursery glasses moments after their entrance into the world. Through their ensuing development, parents and grandparents have been busy getting their pictures in every conceivable situation and from every imaginable pose. Oftentimes my wife and boys spend evenings looking through their picture albums having many chuckles and pleasant memories. My favorite picture of the boys hangs in my study. It is a picture of them dressed in red and white football uniforms with their helmets in their hands. Each time I look at this picture, I can see predictive shades of prospective professional players.

The Bible contains many interesting and treasured portraits of the true and living God. Have you ever stopped to think of your favorite pose of God contained in the Bible? My favorite portrait of God in the Bible is in Luke, chapter fifteen. God's character can be clearly seen in the picture of the father of two sons. "A certain man had two sons" (Luke 15:11).

Many thinkers speak of God as The First Cause, The Divine Energy, or The Prime Mover. These seem to be so impersonal. They represent flash cards of attributes, but they fail to give the biblical revelation of God as a person. No clearer and sharper picture of the Lord can be seen than the disclosure of God as a personal father. The psalmist said, "Like as a father pitieth his children, so the Lord pitieth them that fear him" (Ps. 103:13). "Thou art my father, my God, and the rock of my salvation" (Ps. 89:26). One of Isaiah's names for the Lord was "the everlasting Father" (Isa. 9:6). Jesus taught people to think of God in terms of Father. He told the disciples when they talked to God to address him as, "Our Father which art in heaven " (Luke 11:2). In his parables Jesus frequently used the image of a father to speak about God.

Helmut Thielicke, the great German preacher, labels the picture of God in Luke fifteen with the caption, "The Waiting Father." [1] Without a doubt, this parable communicates many outstanding characteristics of the Lord. This simple story inspired Rembrandt's brush, the music of Debussy, a peom by John Manfield, and even choreographical treatment by Sadler Well's ballet. The central focus in the parable is not the bad behavior of both boys but the loving, gracious attitude the father had toward his two sons. Using this story as a backdrop, let us look at some characteristics of "The Waiting Father."

God's Grief

One day the younger son asked his father, "Father, give me the portion of goods that falleth to me" (Luke 15:12). The father gave the boy his share of the inheritance. Under Jewish law the oldest son received two-thirds of the father's estate, and the youngest son got one-third (cf. Deut. 21:17).

It was not unusual for a father to distribute the estate before his death. Yet, there was something of a callous sound in the younger son's request. It sounded like rebellion.

What do you imagine were the inner feelings of that father when he heard the son's request? Do you think he was glad to get rid of the boy? Do you think the father was mad over this request? Or do you feel there was a deep grief in the father's heart? How you answer this question will determine to a great extent your understanding of God. Use the "focus levers" to allow illumination to come on this picture. Use the "levers" of other revelation from God's word to bring light. Look closer into the story. Put yourself in that father's place. Now with the light from God's word and the illumination from your own feelings, can you not see a brokenhearted father? He was grieved because his son wanted to leave. He was hurt knowing that the son might squander his inheritance. There are certain sorrows which must find vent in tears, else death would be the result. Remember the words of Alfred Lord Tennyson in the beautiful song, "She must weep, or she will die."

God is grieved over humanity's wandering. To get the idea that God is mad over humanity's rebellion is to get a human picture not a biblical portrait of God. Both boys made the father sad. When the younger son left, the father watched the boy depart into the distant horizon until he was gone from sight. A deep grief came to the father because he knew the waste and want which could come to the boy in the far country. The father again was grieved over the self-righteousness of the older boy. Both the sensual and self-righteous sins broke this father's heart. This described the feelings of God. The Lord is grieved over humanity's rebellion whether expressed sensually or self-righteously.

A parent can often understand something about God's grief. In the summer of 1966, we had our first son. When I returned to New Orleans Baptist Theological Seminary in the fall of 1966, I saw one of my professors, Dr. J. Hardee Kennedy. Of course I told him about our new son. Then he responded with an insight I shall never forget. "Harold, we have exposed you to many concepts in the seminary. You have heard much about God, sin, salvation, and other subjects relating to theology and biblical studies. But I have a positive suspicion that you will learn more about how God feels toward human beings as you examine your feelings toward your son." He was exactly right. I learned many Greek and Hebrew words which described God's attitude toward man. I read numerous accounts of God's love in the Bible. But the relationships with my sons have taught me theology in a practical way.

When our boys have rebelled against our desires, the predominant mood has been grief. We have never thrown them out of the house. No, the feelings have been those of undescribable sorrow. During my twenty years of pastoral ministry, I never saw one parent disown his child. Parents have often been exasperated or disappointed, but they have never disowned their child.

The predominant mood of God toward wandering humanity is great grief. Irrespective of the direction of wandering, God hurts because of sin. It wounds the heart and holiness of God. This has been God's mood since the first person's rebellion. When Adam and Eve sinned, one can detect a note of sorrow in God's question, "What is this that thou hast done?" (Gen. 3:13). The generation of Noah grieved the heart of God: "And it repented the Lord that he had made man on the earth, and it grieved him at his heart" (Gen. 6:6). Isaiah characterized God's attitude when he said, "I have nourished and brought up children, and they have rebelled against me" (Isa. 1:2). Hosea understood God's grief. He saw God give birth to Israel as a nation. God taught Israel to walk, and he drew them with "cords of a man, with bands of love" (Hos. 11:4). He protected them as a parent would a child. But Israel had a determination to rebel. Hosea then saw the saddened feelings of God: "How shall I give thee up, Ephraim? how shall I deliver thee, Israel? how shall I make thee as Admah? how shall I set thee as Zeboim? mine heart is turned within me, my repentings are kindled together. I will not execute the fierceness of mine anger, I will not return to destroy Ephraim: for I am God, and not man" (Hos. 11:8–9).

Jesus exposed the feelings of God as the Lord looked on the city of Jerusalem. "O Jerusalem, Jerusalem, which killest the prophets, and stonest them that are sent unto thee; how often would I have gathered thy children together, as a hen doth gather her brood under her wings, and ye would not!" (Luke 13:34).

God grieves over humanity's unfulfilled potential. In the story a great part of the father's grief came because of what the father saw in his son. With his inheritance the boy could have invested in a farm and lived a responsible and useful life. The father lamented over the fact that the boy wasted his substance in riotous living in the far country. He suffered over the boy's lack of meaning and purpose for his life. He agonized over the boy's unhappiness and over the boy's future potential.

Nothing can explain humanity's rebellion. There is no logical explanation for a person's desire to live apart from God. Why would Israel, God's chosen people, reject God's lavished love? Why would Jerusalem, a city full of religious people, not respond to the Lord? Why would a boy choose a far country over a responsible life? In each case, there can be no reasonable answer. People rebel, and in their rebellion they renounce the great possibilities that God has made for them. Nothing makes a parent more sad than a bright, intellectual child to dissipate his intellectual potential. Nothing hurts a father any more than to see a talented child, either musically or athletically, to prodigalize these potentials. Think of God's grief over humanity's squandering of unlimited potential to reflect the glory of God.

God's Interest

After wasting his substance in profligate living, the young son had a desire to return home. Probably he sought to test his father's attitude toward him. He reasoned, "Will my father even allow me to return as a hired servant?" This represented the anxious feelings of the boy.

Turn for a while to the attitude of the father after the son left. Did he dismiss this boy from his mind? Did he regard the boy as rebellious and of little consequence to the family? One expression in the parable gives us a hint about the father's attitude. "But when he was yet a great way off, his father saw him" (Luke 15:20). Evidently the father looked every day for his boy's return. The father never lost interest in his wandering son.

God has an immense interest in all human beings. His interest is personalized. Look closer at the portrait of God in this parable. The father had an individual interest in both boys. Would a father still have an interest in a profligate son who went to the far country? Or would a father take an interest in an obnoxious ostentatious son? The truth of the matter was the father took an individual interest in both boys. He took time to welcome the one that returned. Also, he took time to deal patiently with the self-righteous son. What a tremendous insight this interested father gives of the heavenly Father!

One of the most amazing and incredible persons to live was the great musician, Arturo Toscanini. There is a story that once, just before the orchestra was about to play the evening performance, the bassoon player rushed to the famous conductor and said that he had just discovered that his instrument would not play E-flat. Toscanini held his head in his hands for a few moments and then said: "That will be all right; the note of E-flat does not appear in your music tonight." [2] That was a mark of genius to know the music as intimately as that.

God knows every human being in an intimate way. He is concerned for the masses, but he is also interested in each individual person. The son's question regarding his father's attitude should have been answered by the lavish welcome. The question about the father's attitude can be answered by his individual response to both sons. God takes an immense, individual interest in every person.

God's interest can further be seen by his initiative. As soon as the father caught the faintest glimpse of the returning boy, he moved toward him. He took the initiative. This gesture in the picture could describe an interesting facet of God's character. It suggests that God begins the process of welcoming and restoring wandering human beings. The parables of the lost sheep, the lost coin, and the lost sons depict clearly the seeking love of God. As soon as the father saw the returning son, he ran and before the son could request the status of a slave, the father initiated the welcome as a family member.

God takes the initiative, for he is interested in the return of prodigals. He seeks out sinners and challenges them to a new life-style. The father waited only because the son had to make the choice to return home. As soon as the choice was made, the father ran. Is not Jesus disclosing the initiative of God when he comes to earth?

An interesting experience happened to me in my second pastorate. It was a rural church located in Perry County, Mississippi. In this county, farmers allowed their cattle to roam freely. The county had a law called "The Free Grazing Law." Houses and gardens had to be protected from the roaming livestock. One day a church member rode with me as we drove through a wilderness area. As I drove down the dusty, narrow road, my rider said, "Slow down, preacher!" I thought he was reprimanding me for my fast driving. Then I noticed him as he looked from side to side. "What are you looking for, Reuben?" "I am looking for an old cow that strayed in this area," he replied. "How long has the cow been missing?" I asked. He said, "Oh, I guess about four years." Then I said, "You might as well forget that one." "Preacher," he responded, "I loved that old cow, and I can never just give her up." That conversation taught me that if a man can be that interested in an old cow, how much more interested God is over strayed human beings!

God's Welcome

When the boy returned, the father welcomed him home. The son did not know the results of his decision to return home. He did not know if the father would refuse the desire to be a servant or even if his father would listen to him. He wondered if the father would reprimand him for wasting his inheritance. He thought the father might remind him of the disgrace he had brought to the family. But the boy was surprised over the father's gracious welcome. He never expected the father to restore him to sonship.

God welcomes prodigals! This is the communication of numerous snapshots of God throughout the Bible. No one can read the Bible and point to a picture where God is unwilling to listen and respond to the repentant heart. God's welcome comes as a surprise. No one was more surprised to be received as a son than the prodigal son. The most that he expected was the possibility of being one of the hired servants. Perhaps the sourness of the elder brother originated over the surprise of how his father welcomed the prodigal home. The older son could not fathom the fact that his father welcomed a son who squandered his inheritance and who disgraced the family. Both boys were surprised over their father's welcome.

The scribes and Pharisees were surprised over Jesus' explanation of God. These religious people had a distorted picture of God. They thought that God would only affiliate with "good people." But Jesus received sinners and even ate with them. The scribes and Pharisees were shocked that Jesus would identify with that kind of people and still call himself "the son of God."

Anyone who looks at God's portraits in the gospels is surprised over God's welcome of sinners. I have often been shocked to read of Jesus' response to Zacchaeus, a shrewd tax collector; to a thief dying on a cross, who had stolen from people; to Mary Magdalene, who had slept with numerous men. My human instinct is not to be that receptive. But God welcomes everyone, and I stand in awe of this.

God welcomes prodigals in order to restore them. One must not get the idea that God welcomes with just a liberal acceptance. No, God welcomes people in order to restore them. God welcomes prodigals in order to forgive them of their sins and to give them a life of usefulness. The boy returned from the far country, and the father forgave him. The father made no sharp rebuke. He did not make sure the son had a sufficient sense of guilt. There was no requirement of probation. The father gave no waiting period before accepting his son. When the father forgave and restored, he did it!

The forgiveness of God represents a miracle. It is a miracle that a father would restore a son. It is a greater miracle for God to welcome sinful humanity, cancel their debts, and restore them as responsible children in the family of God. When God receives a person, a miracle takes place. "For this my son was dead, and is alive again; he was lost, and is found" (Luke 15:24). One who has rebelled and killed himself spiritually comes to life. God gives a new life for those who repent.

God's forgiveness is not repair work. It is a real restoration. It means a responsible and joyous life in the family of God. According to this portrait of God, the Lord does not call for an accounting of our rebellious life, but he restores us to an abundant, responsible life.

The picture of "The Waiting Father" is a powerful photograph of God. Without a doubt God placed this portrait into the album so that a world could see him as a holy and eternal Father welcoming and reinstating returning prodigals. One would be foolish to retain an inadequate caricature of God as a rigid bookkeeper, a cruel tyrant, or a localized deity when an authorized photograph of God is available as a loving, waiting, restoring, heavenly Father.

7.
The Fabulous Father

A popular television series several years ago was called "Father Knows Best." Robert Young and Jane Wyatt played the roles of parents with three lively and interesting children. Aside from its entertainment, the weekly programs gave viewers an insight into various factors concerning family living. The producers of the show centered the series around the father. I shared the joys and sorrows of fatherhood. It showed the aspirations, disappointments, and the victories of being a father. Many viewers related to the series for many years, for it portrayed a father in a folksy, personable manner.

The Bible gives us the picture of God as a father. One of the prominent pictures of God in both the Old Testament and the New Testament is that of a father. The Bible speaks in terms of God as a father, but always in the good sense of that term. This term makes God more personable than calling the Lord the first cause or the prime mover. God is referred to as one who is, who speaks, who sees, who hears, who acts, and who loves. The Bible portrays plainly the picture of God as a father.

Jesus taught his disciples to pray, "Our Father which art in heaven" (Matt. 6:9). In the Sermon on the Mount, Jesus taught his followers to think of God as the heavenly Father. "If ye then, being evil, know how to give good gifts unto your children, how much more shall your Father which is in heaven give good things to them that ask him?" (Matt. 7:11).

For Jesus, Father was not just another metaphor for God, but the supreme reality of his own life, an experience of unparalleled intensity and depth.

The picture of God as Father from the Bible should eliminate some foolish notions and erroneous views about God. Many get their idea of God from Greek legends. These pagan stories portray the gods as jealous, vengeful, and grudging. One would not get the picture of a god who wished to help people from these Greek legends. The most significant legend of the gods is the legend of Prometheus. Prometheus was a Greek god, who looked down on earth and took pity on people because they lived without fire. Therefore, Prometheus brought fire to earth and gave it for cheer and comfort. Zeus, king of the gods, was angry that man should receive the gift of fire. Zeus took Prometheus and chained him to a rock in the middle of the Adriatic Sea, where he was tortured with the heat and thirst of the day, and the cold of night. Zeus prepared a vulture to tear out the liver of Prometheus, which always grew again, only to be torn out again. This represents the pagan concept of what happens to a god who seeks to help people.

The picture of God in the Bible is one who possesses the name and heart of a father. When we learn of God as a father, we do not shiver in fear. Instead, we rest in his love and look at the biblical picture for greater insight into "Our Father which art in heaven" (Matt. 6:9).

A Father Knows His Children

Think for a moment about an earthly father. Any decent father would know the name of each of his children. Most fathers even remember the birthdays of each child. Have you ever seen an average father who had difficulty remembering the name of one of his children? Even if a father had a dozen children, he would know the identity of each child.

A good earthly father knows more about his child than

mere identity. He knows particular traits and qualities about the child that perhaps the child does not know about himself. A father knows that one son has a fiery temper and the other son keeps his feelings inward. A father knows the son's proclivity to rebel openly against the wishes of his mother. The same father may know the daughter's tendency to obey outwardly but to hate obedience within her inner being. An earthly father knows distinctives, traits, and tendencies of his children.

How much more does the heavenly Father know his children? One of the most amazing qualities of God's nature is that he knows each individual who lives, who has ever lived, and who will live by name. In addition to an identifiable knowledge, God has an intimate knowledge about each person. God knows us. He knows our names. He knows our sorrows. He knows our aspirations. He knows our failures. To be sure, the heavenly Father knows best.

The heavenly Father shows us his personableness. The picture of God as father shows us that God is not something but someone. He is not an idea known in abstract nouns and adjectives such as "The Supreme Being, Providence, Absolute Wisdom, Power, Justice." God is a person.

In the Old Testament God spoke of himself with the personal pronoun "I." In the New Testament God came in a person. Of course the word person does not fully describe God. Yet, we would not be satisfied with flash cards of impersonal and abstract words. To speak of God as a person embodies ideas that are important when we speak of God. Throughout the Bible God reveals himself in personal ways as "Father," "Son," "Holy Spirit."

To speak of God as a heavenly Father shows us a God who is above us, beyond us, and different from us. Yet, to speak of God as the heavenly Father tells us that God draws near to us and makes himself known in an intimate way. He wishes to help and to be our companion. Throughout the Bible we learn about the personal qualities of the heavenly Father to be loving, gracious, merciful, patient, forgiving, and just. God is a preeminent and personal heavenly Father. He is not an impersonal abstraction known by appellations as "The Moral Law," "The Prime Mover." No, when one speaks in these vague generalities about God's self-revelation, it is not the picture of the Bible. The Bible pictures God as Father— infinitely above human beings but intimately related to human beings.

God is our heavenly Father. Not a principle, not a force, but a person, and not just any kind of a person, but a father. Look at the very best human father you can imagine. God is infinitely, fabulously more.

The heavenly Father demonstrates an intimate interest in his children. Because God is near us, he is intimately interested and concerned for our welfare. Any earthly father worthy of note takes an interest in his children. He rejoices when his children excel in athletics, in scholastics, or in any other area. The father grieves when a child fails in something or strays away from the family intention. Any good earthly father takes the closest interest in his children's welfare and activities.

Looking back over my life, I can see the immense involvement of my father in my life. He was interested in football practice after school. He took an interest when I was in a play. When I suffered from an accident, he was interested enough to drive miles to be with me. The Sunday I preached my first sermon, he was interested. Even when I was ticketed for speeding, he took a close interest.

If an earthly father takes such an interest, think how much more interest the heavenly Father has for us. The heavenly Father is not capricious. He is not sometimes loving and interested and sometimes unloving and disinterested. Everything that everyone does comes under God's interest. The heavenly Father takes a special interest in each child.

A Father Hears His Children

Look closer into the picture of God as a heavenly Father. Further investigation yields the idea that a good earthly father takes the time to listen to one of his children. The father longs to hear the first sounds of his child. He takes pride when he hears the child's first utterance of "Da Da." The father listens to the increasing vocabulary of his child and then to the formation of sentences. A good father listens to the youngsters imaginative conversations. Then he listens to the "rapping" of teenagers. The father then has to hear the sophisticated and scholastic conversation of the college student. All throughout his lifetime, the father is a listener.

Think about the importance of an earthly father taking the time to listen to his children. It demonstrates attentiveness and an attempt to understand the child. Think of all the variety of conversations a father listens to during parenthood: the high-pitched conversations filled with joy; and the soft tones of sadness; the tones of bitterness and disappointment; the aspiring conversations filled with ambitious dreams; the daily, informational conversations.

The heavenly Father listens attentively. If a good earthly father listens to his children, think how much more the heavenly Father is attentive to his children. One of the greatest qualities about God in the Bible is that he listens attentively. During the days of Egyptian captivity, God heard the cries of his children. "I have surely seen the affliction of my people which are in Egypt, and have heard their cry by reason of their taskmasters; for I know their sorows" (Ex. 3:7). The psalmist was convinced that God heard him. "The Lord will hear when I call unto him" (Ps. 4:3). "In my distress I called upon the Lord, and cried unto my God: he heard my voice out of his temple, and my cry came before him, even unto his ears" (Ps. 18:6). The prophet Micah affirmed his belief that God listened attentively to him. "I will wait for the God of my salvation: my God will hear me" (Mic. 7:7).

Every person can talk to an attentive God. He is not too busy with more important cosmic affairs to listen to each child. He is not too concerned about larger and more significant matters than your petty problems. One of the greatest truths about God is that he is aware of me, hears what I say, and attends to my needs.

The heavenly Father listens understandingly. The heavenly Father goes deeper than mere listening. He listens with understanding. He knows our motives when we talk to him. He understands the circumstances out of which we speak.

Jesus had an unforgettable manner of giving pictures of God in understandable images. He believed earthly and human analogies could help people know God's nature and will. Jesus had a way of saying, "Take the very best father you know among humans. God is all that—and fabulously more!" Recall his illustration of the asking son: "Or what man is there of you, whom if his son ask bread, will he give him a stone? Or if he ask a fish, will he give him a serpent?" (Matt. 7:9–10). Jesus gave the picture of God listening to man with deep understanding. We can trust the God who understands us. The disciple with an understanding heavenly Father will open his heart with utter freeness. He will also be able to accept whatever God sends, believing that the all-wise and all-loving God understands his children better than they know themselves.

Our pediatrician first taught us to listen with understanding to our baby's cries. He talked to us about the various ways a baby communicates in crying. One cry could be detected as a hunger call. Another tone could be determined as an attention getter. Then another cry different from the previous two was a cry from illness. My wife and I finally learned to understand our children's needs by the way they cried.

Think how much more God understands us. He knows why we ask, he knows what we ask, he knows what we need. No one understands us or our cries as our heavenly Father does.

A Father Corrects His Children

Look closer into the traits and qualities of an earthly father. When you do a close investigation of a good father, you will inevitably see the quality of discipline. Good fathers rear their children with discipline. It helps the child grow into their authentic and best self.

No good father exercises punishment to harm the child. The good father does not discipline the child out of his own frustrations. He does not take out his own inner hostilities on the child. Instead, an earthly father disciplines children for their betterment. It breaks them of bad habits and helps them form good habits. It frees them from harmful traits of character and forms helpful qualities of life. Because the father knows what is best for the child, he subjects the child to correction.

Seeing correction to be a prominent trait of an earthly father convinces us that the heavenly Father corrects his children. The Bible portrays God as correcting his children. "For whom the Lord loveth he correcteth; even as a Father the son in whom he delighteth" (Prov. 3:12). God revealed himself to Israel as a loving Father who disciplined them. "Thou shalt also consider in thine heart, that, as a man chasteneth his son, so the Lord thy God chasteneth thee" (Deut. 8:5). The psalmist delighted in God's correction. "Blessed is the man whom thou chastenest, O Lord, and teachest him out of thy law" (Ps. 94:12).

Without question the heavenly Father exercises the discipline of correction. "My son, despise not thou the chastening of the Lord, nor faint when thou art rebuked of him: For whom the Lord loveth he chasteneth, and scourgeth every son whom he receiveth (Heb. 12:5–6).

God corrects a child with the nature of love. God is love. One must never see God's discipline as being opposite from his love. God is never to be considered as sometimes loving and sometimes correcting. He is not to be seen at one moment kind with gifts and the next moment unkind with correction. Our Father in heaven has the nature of love, and whenever he corrects a child it issues from love.

Any concept of the heavenly Father correcting from any nature other than love is insufficient. J. B. Phillips in his book *Your God Is Too Small* points to the erroneous view of God as a policeman. God is not an awesome administrator deserving to hold up law at the expense of human life and welfare.

The Bible does not give a picture of a revenge-seeking tyrant or a judge trapped helplessly by his responsibility to enforce an impersonal law of his own making. It tells of a Father who corrects out of a nature of love. "For whom the Lord loveth he chasteneth, and scourgeth every son whom he receiveth" (Heb. 12:6). Try to imagine the most loving earthly father you know. Think of how he would correct his child. You conclude that he corrects his child. You conclude that he corrects his child out of a heart of love. How much more does God chasten out of love.

The word "chastening" from Hebrews 12:6 comes from *paideuo* which means "to train a child." So the chastening of the heavenly Father does not spring from a nature of revenge. It comes from a loving heavenly Father.

God corrects his children for the interest of the family. No one would respect an earthly father who exerted no form of discipline. The more we look at the picture of God as a Father who corrects his children the more we respect and revere the Lord. The Lord disciplines children not for their injury or their harm, but for their ultimate and highest good. Correcting a child ultimately leads to their greatest benefit. It will enhance their effectiveness and happiness as an individual child of God.

God corrects individuals to promote the welfare of the entire family. A father might have six children. Because of the error of one the happiness and welfare of the entire family can be impaired. Consequently, the father would correct the child both for the child's individual good and for the corporate happiness in the family.

God corrects to protect the family name. When a child misbehaves before other people, whose reputation is injured? Isn't the good name of the parents held in question? When a father allows his child to pull books off my shelves and damage my furniture, I think less of that father. The father has a parental duty to establish and maintain a good family name. God wants to maintain a good name in his family, therefore he corrects his children.

A Father Meets His Children's Needs

Any good human father will meet the needs of his children. In the rearing of a child, a father responds naturally to the various needs of a child. The father provides the various physical needs. A child cannot get food, clothing, and shelter. The good father looks out for these needs and provides them for the child. As a child grows older, mental needs have to be met. Fathers send their sons and daughters to school in order to acquaint them with the world about them. All throughout early childhood and adolescence fathers will meet various emotional needs of the child. This supplies one of the greatest needs of life, a support for the emotions.

Knowing that an earthly father meets the needs of his children teaches a great truth about God. Throughout God's picture album, he reveals himself as a father who provides for the needs of his children. During Israel's Exodus from Egypt and sojourn in the wilderness, God provided for their needs. "For the Lord thy God hath blessed thee in all the works of thy hand: he knoweth thy walking through this great wilderness: these forty years the Lord thy God hath been with thee; thou hast lacked nothing" (Deut. 2:7). The psalmist said, "The Lord is my shepherd; I shall not want" (Ps. 23:1). Jesus taught the disciples to pray for their needs which included provisions for the day, pardon for their sins, and protection of their loyalty to the heavenly Father. The Bible pictures God as the heavenly Father who takes care of his children's needs.

The picture of God meeting human needs gives an insight into the nature of God. Jesus told two parables—the friend at midnight and the importunate widow. He artistically painted an unforgettable picture of God. He enabled people to know the nature of the giving God in these two parables. The first story is about a disobeying neighbor. Late one night a friend turned up unexpectedly at a friend's house and caught him without food in the cupboard. The householder went to the neighbor's house and knocked asking for three loaves which was the usual meal for one person.

In ancient Palestine most houses had one room. The householder's children were bedded in that room. The hammering on the door awakened the householder. The householder called to the figure in the dark to go away. Getting up would disturb his children. But the visitor persisted in knocking. He kept on knocking till at last in sheer exasperation the neighbor got up, unbolted the door, and gave him three loaves of bread.

The second story tells of a poor widow whose opponent refused to settle a debt. She kept coming to the judge and demanding, "Give me justice against my oppressor." The judge did nothing at first. Day after day she kept on asking the judge for justice. Finally the judge gave in to the cries of the widow and gave her justice.

The Lord taught the nature of the giving God by the use of contraries. The point is "How much greater is God!" People do not have to plead with God as with an indifferent neighbor or a callous, insensitive judge. God is not like the neighbor or the judge. He is like the loving father, only infinitely more loving. We can trust his goodness and do not need to bother or to tease him in order for our needs to be met, whether the daily physical provision or justice.

The two parables also give an insight into how God meets our needs. We have seen that God is pictured as a father rather than an indifferent neighbor or an insensitive judge. But how does a father give? Does he give by our persistent begging? Is that the way God gives? If we keep on asking will God get tired and give us what we ask? No, this is not the way a father gives. My boys have been asking me for a motorcycle for years. They have been persistent. Will I ultimately relent to their request out of their lingering desire and persistent request? No, I do not feel that a motorcycle would be in the best interest of my boys. My refusal is based on their best interest rather than my unexplainable refusal.

How does God give? The answer is simple. How God gives is seen in the picture of an earthly father, yet much greater. A father gives gifts to children not from intensive and persistent petitions. God provides for his children out of their needs and what would be best for their lives.

God is not a cosmic Santa Claus giving gifts to asking children. He is a loving Father who knows his children's needs and meets them in their best interest. A father meets the needs of children with perfect wisdom and perfect love. Fathers refuse many children's wishes but not real needs. God answers our petitions in the way that it would be best for us. Giving children their desires could be the worst thing for them. God answers his children's needs in the way that is best for them.

If men, with all their evil seek the best for their children, how much more will God give what is best to his children. The answer God gives is always based on love for us and wisdom for what is best for us.

8.
The Forgiving Father

As you look through a person's picture album, you can easily see favorite poses. By now you can see that my favorite portrait of God is that of a father. Already I have shown snapshots of "The Waiting Father" and "The Fabulous Father." Now I want to show you the angle of "The Forgiving Father." This picture does not reflect a different heavenly Father. It is just an enlargement of one special feature of his nature. This blowup of the heavenly Father will focus on the trait of God's marvelous forgiveness.

Earthly fathers have unique traits which receive prominent attention. Some fathers have the ability to excel in their work. Children delight in their father's special skills. Through the years I have marveled over my dad's ability to sell. I have coveted his ability to meet the public and to sell them what they need. Some fathers possess physical abilities. Sons single out fathers who can jog two or three miles or can still hit a home run with a baseball. Other fathers possess abilities to understand and to counsel their children. Sons respond to fathers who listen and guide them wisely. Girls also rejoice in their dad's ability to listen, to understand, and to guide. Fathers are something special.

If earthly fathers are special, how much more special is the heavenly Father! No picture album is large enough to hold the enlargement of the distinctive traits and qualities of the heavenly Father. Our heavenly Father is strong enough to create a universe out of nothing. Earthly fathers can make a chair out of a tree, but the heavenly Father can make a tree. Look at the loving nature of the Father. He loves in spite of unworthy children. With love and understanding the Father listens to his children and guides them with wisdom. Look closely at the enlargement of the Father's holiness. He is pure, without sin, and righteous. You can look at every facet of the heavenly Father, but you will never find a flaw in his character. Focus upon the good deeds which the Father does for the children. Out of a gracious nature of love, the heavenly Father acts to redeem and to save his children from their selfish behavior. By the sending of Jesus to earth, he acted to reconcile erring children and bring them back to God, to personal wholeness, and to healthy relationships with others. There are so many special qualities of the heavenly Father that one cannot focus upon all of them. The Almighty Father, the one and only God, is special!

Amid the many traits that I have observed of the heavenly Father, I want to look at one enlargement. It is a blowup of God's forgiveness in Luke 15. Of all the traits of the father, nothing fascinates me more than to see his nature to forgive. This father had two sons, and both of them were rebellious. The younger son left home to express his rebellion in sensual living. The older son stayed home, but he was self-righteous and unloving toward the father and his brother. The amazing fact is the father's willingness to forgive. What a picture of God to see a father welcoming a prodigal son! What a picture of God to see a father dealing patiently and graciously with a self-righteous, grumbling son! Let's focus on the heavenly Father's special qualities of forgiveness.

God Absorbs Hurts

To understand something of the nature of God, we can look closely into what happens when he forgives. When the prodigal son returned from the far country, the father received him. He lavished gifts upon him which symbolized his acceptance. Without a doubt the father had been deeply wounded. A son had squandered his inheritance. Another son had lived at home, but there was no inward commitment. The father was embarrassed over the action of the prodigal. Any way you look at this story, the father was profoundly hurt.

When the son came home, the father forgave him. Did this mean that the hurt left immediately? Or did the hurt prevent the father's forgiveness? "No," is the answer to both questions. The father's wounded feelings and injured reputation did not prevent his action of forgiveness. Of course the hurt caused by the son did not leave immediately. The father absorbed the hurt.

The heavenly Father absorbs the hurt inflicted by rebellious human beings. The younger son injured his father in numerous ways. He abused his father's gifts. Nothing is sadder than a person who abuses his privileges. Israel, the chosen nation of God, had numerous blessings lavished upon them. But they abused these blessings. Nothing brought more grief to the heavenly Father than Israel's actions.

During the days of Jesus' ministry on earth, people possessed the opportunity to see God in the flesh. But they also abused the privilege. Nonetheless, Jesus demonstrated magnanimity when he forgave those who injured him.

The younger son of Luke 15 also abandoned the father's hope. The father had high intentions for that boy. He wanted him to inherit the estate and carry on the family business as any Jewish boy was intended to do. When the boy left home, he abandoned the high hopes of the father. One could not imagine the inward grief suffered by this conscientious and ambitious father. A son had broken his heart.

Think of the hurt of the heavenly Father. Human beings, the crown of God's creation, break the heart of God. They have been ungrateful for his gifts. They have rebelled against his intention. They have been arrogantly rebellious against

God's will. No one can imagine the grief of God over his wayward children.

The heavenly Father absorbs the hurt when children repent. The amazing character of God is displayed in a father who was willing to receive a wayward boy. In forgiving the boy, the father had to take the hurt within himself. The forgiving, heavenly Father has to absorb the hurt inflicted by our rebellion. What a great Father who is willing to absorb the hurt in order for children to be forgiven!

God's absorption of our sin means that he forgets. After the boy returned from the far country, the father accepted him and did not interrogate him about the far country. The father did not want to know about his episodes. More than likely, he never mentioned the far country. In absorbing the hurt, the father forgot his years of rebellion.

How much greater does God forget our sins! Three Old Testament words are used to describe God's forgiveness. The word *kipper* means "a covering." The word *nasa* means "to lift up and carry away." Then the word *salach* means "to let go." All three words describe the gesture of God's forgiveness. Sin is covered, and it no longer obtrudes between man and God. It is carried away no longer to form a barrier. It is forgiven so there resides no resentment in the injured party. "As far as the east is from the west, so far hath he removed our transgressions from us" (Ps. 103:12). "I, even I, am he that blotteth out thy transgressions for mine own sake, and will not remember thy sins" (Isa. 43:25). Nathan said about the atrocious actions of David, "The Lord also hath put away thy sin" (2 Sam. 12:13). The heavenly Father is willing to forgive and to remember the transgressor's sin no more. He is willing to absorb the hurt.

God Cancels Debts

Volumes could be written about the father who forgave his son. A father running to meet a returning prodigal son gives us a glimpse of what the heavenly Father feels toward sinners. The father embracing and kissing the wretched son gives us a picture of how God thinks about us. The father giving the returning shoes for his sons's feet, rings for his hand, and a feast for fellowship communicates that the father had canceled the debt.

One of the greatest truths about God is that he cancels the debts of sinners. The New Testament has a word for sin which is *opheilema*. This is the word Jesus used in the Model Prayer, "And forgive us our debts, as we forgive our debtors" (Matt. 6:12). It means a debt. Consequently, sin means a failure to pay that which is due. There can be no person who will ever dare to claim that he has fulfilled perfectly his duty to God and to his fellowman.

God forgives enormous debts. Everyone has failed in his duty to God and to other people. Some have failed in a greater way than others. Nonetheless, every person has failed to pay that which is due the Lord and our fellowman. The truth of the matter is that we cannot pay our debts.

The prodigal son owed an enormous debt to his father and to his brother. He failed in his duty as a responsible son to follow the father's intention. He disgraced the father's reputation with the loose living in the far country. He failed in his duty to his older brother, even though he was a self-righteous brother. He was in great debt to his father and to his brother.

What did the father do about this son's enormous debt? The story makes it clear. He canceled his son's debt. This is what God does to debtors. He forgives. In the New Testament there are three Greek words translated "forgiveness, *apoluō*—"to loose away," *charizomai*—to "be gracious," and *aphiemi*—to "send away." Frank Stagg says that the basic idea of forgiveness in the New Testament is "that of canceling a debt—the removal of the barrier to reconciliation, the banishing of the sin." [1]

The forgiving Father cancels enormous debts. One of the most graphic pictures of God's magnanimous forgiveness was told in a simple story of Jesus. It was about a king who held a day of reckoning with his servants. One servant owed a debt which ran into the millions. The king was about to cast the servant into prison and sell his wife and family to collect part of the debt. But the servant pled pathetically, and the king canceled his enormous debt. We shall look at the rest of the story later, but now lets focus upon the graciousness of the king. This king forgave an enormous debt which the servant could not pay. He averted disaster for the servant. No logic or reason can explain the gesture other than the amazing benevolence and graciousness of a king. This is a picture of God. He cancels debts which cannot be paid by human beings. Without logic or reason God forgives. He is gracious and willing to cancel our debts.

God cancels debts from a gracious disposition, not mathematics. That which motivated Jesus' story of the forgiving king was Peter's question. "Lord, how oft shall my brother sin against me, and I forgive him? till seven times?" (Matt. 18:21). The rabbis drew pictures of God from the basis of a mathematical perspective. They taught that God extended forgiveness up to three offenses. After the third offense God visited with punishment. Peter thought that he had a better picture of God. He took the rabbinical formula, multiplied it by two, and added one for good measure. Peter in essence said, "I have a great picture of God as a marvelous forgiver. He will forgive up to seven times!"

Then Jesus told Peter how God forgives. "I say not unto thee, Until seven times: but, Until seventy times seven (Matt. 18:22). Then Jesus illustrated the statement about the servant who owed his master an enormous debt, and the king forgave. He forgave out of his gracious character. Humanly speaking, he should not have forgiven.

Mathematically speaking, God should not forgive anyone.

Our debts to God are so great. Our resources to repay are so inadequate. But God is not the great mathematician. He is the great forgiving Father. He exercises magnanimous unlimited forgiveness.

God Restores Relationships

The picture of God as the forgiving father does not merely portray a father speaking momentous words of forgiveness. A father welcomes home his returning son. If the gracious welcome were not enough sign of restoration, the father gave more evidences of receiving his son. He gave the boy a ring for his hands and shoes for his feet. Both of these articles had a family significance. Slaves did not wear shoes, and sons often wore family rings. The father proved to the boy that he was not a slave but a son.

The heavenly Father's forgiveness is more than a gracious speech. It is far more than a mechanical transaction of canceling a debt. Forgiveness is not the gesture of a mighty mathematician or a benevolent bookkeeper. It is the act of a heavenly Father. God cancels the debts of rebellious prodigals, and these forgiven children are brought into a wondrous relationship with God and with his family. Therefore, our picture of God is not one of a calculative computer giving readouts of forgiveness. It is of a father restoring children.

God restores people to a relationship with him. The great tragedy of wandering humanity is the alienation from God that results from their rebellion. The prodigal son went to the far country. During his daydreaming, the far country promised exciting pleasures, but the life in the far country failed to satisfy his deep longings and needs. Having chosen to leave home and to live away from the father's house, the boy created a gap between his father and himself. He was away from home, alienated from his father. He longed to return home even if it meant to be a hired servant.

Wandering humanity has alienated itself from God. Because of stubborn selfishness, human beings refuse to obey the Father's wishes. This rebellion estranges them from the God who loves them, wants to have fellowship with them, and wants to look after their highest good. The prodigal son experienced the miseries of life away from the father's house. It meant to be isolated, lonely, and to possess a deep sense of not really belonging. Added to these feelings was the attitude of hostility. It involved a deep distrust of others. The prodigal son probably thought that his father would not receive him back, so he asked for a servant's role. Alienated human beings get the picture that God is their adversary rather than a gracious Father who desires to restore a relationship.

The picture of God is not an enemy but a forgiving Father. He seeks to bring strayed human beings into a right relationship with him. The father demonstrated no hesitancy in making the prodigal a restored son. He didn't want to get even with his son. The predominant pose of God throughout the Bible is of one seeking to remove the alienation and to restore strayed persons. "And you, that were sometimes alienated and enemies in your mind by wicked works, yet now hath he reconciled" (Col. 1:21). To reconcile means to heal or to reestablish a broken relationship. The term reconciliation was used in the first century to mean the mending of a broken marriage. It was used to describe a couple getting back together after a period of separation. The Bible never speaks of God being reconciled to man. It is human beings who need to be reconciled to God.

To be forgiven means to be in a new relationship with God. What a marvelous insight to see God willing to take wandering, rebellious, erring human beings and call them his children. Forgiveness means to be in a new relationship with God.

God restores relationships with others. The father created a new relationship with his prodigal son. This brought a new relationship with the family. More than likely the forgiving father wanted his son to be a forgiver. He had been extended forgiveness by his father, and the father expected him to forgive the same way.

God expects his forgiven children to forgive on the basis of how they have been forgiven. Freely they have received, freely they should forgive their fellowman. Now let us go back to the story of the merciful king recorded in Matthew 18:23–35. No sooner had the king canceled the debt of the servant than the servant met people who owed him a debt. The debtor pled with the servant for patience; the servant refused and had the debtor jailed. When the king heard of this action, he shared his indignation: "You scoundrel! I canceled your enormous debt when you begged for mercy. Were you not to show the same attitude as I showed you?"

God gives wandering humanity a new relationship, and he places upon them the responsibility to forgive. God expects us to "Be merciful even as your Father also is merciful" (Luke 6:36). God does not keep office ledgers. He is "our Father." If a person says, "I'll never forgive you," then that person has hardly known God as the Father who forgives. In one of the legends associated with Leonardo da Vinci, the artist is said to have painted his enemy's face on the shoulders of Judas, and, the story goes, he could not conjure up the face of Christ. But when he forgave his enemy and painted out the insult, he saw Christ's face. The question is: "Are the children of God willing to resemble the nature of their Father and practice magnanimous forgiveness?"

The portrait of God as a forgiving Father helps us with our concept of the Lord. God does not take sin lightly, and he does not eliminate it with some religious, mechanical transaction. Forgiveness is possible only by one who is morally sensitive and deeply grieved, and who is willing to bear, to cancel, and to give all that the wanderer may be won back to life.

9.
The Weed Exterminator

In the fifteenth century an artist worked on a picture of the face of Jesus. When the artist finished his first sketch of the face of the Redeemer, he called in his landlady's little daughter and asked her who she thought it was. The little girl looked at it and said, "It is a good man." The painter knew that he had failed. He destroyed the first sketch, and after praying for greater skill he finished a second. Again he called the little girl and asked her to tell him who she thought the face represented. This time the girl thought it looked like a great sufferer. Again the painter knew that he had failed, and again he destroyed the sketch he had made. After meditation and prayer, a third sketch was made. When it was finished, he called the girl in a third time and asked her who it was. Looking at the portrait, the girl knelt down and exclaimed, "It is the Lord!"

Reading the parable commonly known as the wheat and the tares in Matthew 13:24–30 resembles something of the girl and the artist. The first reading might yield the conclusion: "It is a parable of wheat and tares." Reading the parable closer might yield the conclusion: "It is a parable depicting the ultimate triumph of righteousness over unrighteousness." Close study and intensive reading of the parable yields the conclusion: "It is a picture of the Lord!"

The parable tells about a man who sowed good seed in his field. While the man slept, his enemy came and sowed tares among the wheat. The weed was the poisonous bearded darnel which was regarded as a perverted kind of wheat. The servants of the householder expressed concern over the growth of the tares with the wheat. They wanted to pick out the weeds. The owner told the servants to allow both to grow together until the harvest day. On that day the wheat could be separated from the tares. The wheat would be gathered into the barn, and the tares would be destroyed.

Interpreters of this parable have gotten many ideas from this simple story. The story contains the mystery of wickedness. It depicts a termination of time. It reveals the presence of good and evil together. It could give a glimpse of judgment at the end of history.

Irrespective of the numerous truths which one could extract from this simple parable of Jesus, a picture of God as The Weed Exterminator or The Great Harvester can be seen clearly. "He that soweth the good seed is the Son of man" (Matt. 13:37). Jesus' explanation of the wheat and tares explicitly relates that within this parable one can see a portrait of God.

Look in the parable and see the Great Harvester. God performs mighty works. This is represented by the farmer sowing good seed. Amid the good works of God, an enemy sows discord. This is clearly depicted with the tares. Yet, the presence of wickedness does not usurp the power of God. There will be a harvest day. God can distinguish good from evil. God will someday exterminate evil from human living. Look closely into the parable and discover some great truths about God.

God's Intention

The act of the sower planting good seed gives an insight into the nature and character of God. It gives an insight into God's intention. A closer look into the picture of God depicted in the parable will give an insight into what God intends to do and is doing for the world. God is responsible for sowing good seed. He does not sow the tares or the evil. An enemy must be blamed for this serious misfortune. From the parable we learn a great truth prominent throughout the Bible, and that is God does not intend evil for people. He intends good for human beings.

Oftentimes people present a false picture of God when they talk about "the will of God." The Bible does not present the revelation of God as malicious deity. Neither does the Bible portray the Lord with iron determinism. Leslie Weatherhead in his book entitled *The Will of God* writes about "God's Intentional Will." He calls upon his audience to dissociate from the phrase "the will of God" all that is evil and unpleasant and unhappy. Weatherhead says, "The intentional will of God means the way in which God pours himself out in goodness, such as the true father longs to do for his son." [1]

Thomas Hardy finished his novel *Tess* with the grim words: "The President of the Immortals had finished his sport with Tess." Hardy did not get this picture of God from the Bible regarding God's intention. He got this from his own distorted reasonings. John Greenleaf Whittier said:

> I know not where His islands lift
> Their fronded palms in air;
> I only know I cannot drift
> Beyond His love and care.

Any concept which does not conceive of God intending the best for humanity does not come from the Bible. Let us get our idea of what God intends from the Bible.

God intends a lovely and ordered universe. God made the world to pour out his goodness to humanity. After each phase of God's creation, an assessment was made. "And God saw that it was good" (cf. Gen. 1:10,12,21,25). In the creation God did not give misery, unhappiness, disappointment, and frustration.

From the beginning God created a lovely and ordered universe. God made the natural beauty of earth, sky, and sea for humanity's enjoyment. He ordained the various natural laws not to detain human beings but to enable them to live an ordered life on earth. The creation of God was no cosmic trick which lead to humanity's unhappiness. Instead, all of God's creation represents the Lord's treat which leads to mankind's happiness.

The creation account discloses the intention of the Lord. He intended a lovely and ordered universe. Anything that robs life of beauty and orderliness does not issue from God. It comes from man's selfishness and the satanic enemy. The parable says, "An enemy hath done this."

God intends harmonious relationships. God made mankind to have fellowship and companionship with the Lord and to enjoy the world. The creation account in Genesis discloses a God who desired to walk in the garden with Adam and Eve. The account of God's redemption after man had sinned discloses a God who continues to want to relate to erring humanity. Any ideas contrary to this truth do not come from biblical photographs but imaginative drawings of God from human hands. God sows good seed. The children of the kingdom sow good seed, seeking to establish mankind back in a harmonious relationship with God. Any sowing of discord comes either from the self-centeredness of a person or from "the enemy."

God intends a harmonious and happy relationship with fellow human beings. God intends for the world to live together in a harmonious relationship. The Bible discloses a God who seeks to find rebellious human beings, make them into new creations so they can live together in the world as a family. The figure of sowing the good seed in the parable speaks of God's intention to redeem man with the gospel. This will have an individual transformation which will effect a person's relationship with other human beings. Discord and animosity between human beings does not represent God's intention. It represents human selfishness and the work of an enemy.

God's Permission

In addition to the insight about God's intention from this parable, one can also see God's permission. The man had sowed his field with good seed. But while everyone was asleep, his enemy came and sowed darnel (weedy grasses, tares). The farmer's men came to him. "Sir," they said, "was it not good seed you sowed in your field? Then where has the darnel come from?" "This is the enemy's work," he replied. "Then," they asked, "shall we go and gather the darnel?" "No," he answered, "in gathering it up, you might pull up the wheat at the same time. Let them both grow together till the harvest; and at the harvest time I will tell the reapers, 'gather the darnel first and tie it in bundles, then collect the wheat into my barn.' "

Amid the beautiful background of God's high intention for the world comes the enemy on to the scene. The story confronts us with the stubborn fact and mystery of evil in a God-created world. Jesus did not elaborate on the identity of the enemy. Whether the enemy of the field was Satan, or ingrained perversity of human choice, or some other antagonism, is not answered. The greatest question seems to be, "Why does God allow an enemy to sow discord in the world?"

Looking closer into the parable yields the conclusion that evil is not in the world by the will of God. The story plainly says that the tares were due to "an enemy." This fact would help some people clear up their concept of God. Quite often people attribute numerous atrocious happenings to the "will of God." Obviously the act of sowing tares in our world is not the work of the loving, almighty Father. It is the work of the sinister character known as Satan.

Numerous questions arise about the evil in our world. When did this evil originate? Why does God allow such a sinister power in our world? Various explanations have been given regarding evil. First, some say that there is a good God and there is an evil god. This is a relative dualism. The Bible does not present Satan as a second god. The Bible presents God who alone is God and has no rival comparable to him. Second, others insist that evil comes from God himself. They reason that God created everything, then he must be the creator of evil, too. Unquestionably, the Bible teaches that God is against evil. Consequently, we cannot say God is the author of evil.

Third, some say evil originates from within a person. Some say that evil springs from within a person's body or mind. Hence, evil is a human creation according to this view. Fourth, others contend that evil can be identified as fallen angels. They base this view on Isaiah 14:12; 2 Peter 2:4; Jude 6; and Revelation 12:7–9. This contends that Satan led a rebellion in heaven and was cast out. This creates a problem on how a good heaven could be perverted with evil.

Even though we have looked at various explanations of the origin of evil, no explanation is sufficient. No one can explain the origin and fact of evil in God's good world. The Genesis story makes no attempt to tell where the tempter came from or why he exists in God's world.

Perhaps the best explanation of evil in God's good world is that it exists under the permissive will of God. The truth we see is that an enemy works constantly to sabotage and to oppose the work of God. The work of the enemy was included to demonstrate that evil is represented as being ultimately contrary to the will of God. Evil exists only with the permission of God.

God has preeminence over evil. The parable makes it clear that God's toleration is only temporary. All through the process of the enemy sowing tares, God could intervene.

God has the ability to distinguish between the wheat and the tares. No one else has that ability. God knows the difference between the good and bad now. The parable portrays a preeminent, all-knowing God. We are cautioned against the fact that we can try to play the part of God by presuming to know who belongs to the Lord. God alone knows the heart. Only god possesses that preeminent knowledge. Only God possesses the right to judge. God can destroy evil at any time. He has absolute preeminence over the enemy.

God's Vindication

The parable teaches about the God who judges. It teaches us that God will vindicate his way in the world. The farmer allowed the wheat and the tares to grow together. But he announced to his laborers. "Let both grow together until the harvest: and in the time of harvest I will say to the reapers, 'Gather ye together first the tares, and bind them in bundles to burn them: but gather the wheat into my barn' "(Matt. 13:30).

One must not infer the wrong picture of God from this parable. To leave off the earlier part of the story and to emphasize too strongly the judgment of God would be a mistake. Let us not just see a tolerant God who overlooks the sowing of evil. Also, let us not see just a vindicative God of judgment. Look at the totality of the story. It portrays a patient loving God who sought to fulfill his intention during the course of history. Yet, this same God, patient and loving comes to a time of vindication, a time of judgment. God will ultimately be a weed exterminator. In today's world many people regard the notion of a final sifting of unrighteous people from the righteous as just a fairy tale from the Bible. If this is so, it only shows that people presume upon themselves to be better informed on God than Jesus himself.

Robert Burns told the rigidly righteous people of his day about judging.

> Who made the heart, 'tis He alone
> Decidedly can try us,
> He knows each chord, the vibrant tone,
> Each spring, its various bias.

The job of sifting does not belong to mortals. It is a task appropriate only for eternal omniscience for the great knower of hearts, for the great harvester.

God judges according to differences. The farmer told the servants to wait until the harvest day for the separation of the tares from the wheat. The harvest day will be a time when the wheat and the tares will be manifest for what they are. One cannot look with suspicion upon the farmer for making this separation. Actually, the farmer makes a distinction according to the nature of the particular crop.

Think about the weed exterminator. Through the long troublesome course of history, he has been patient with the agitation of the enemy. The weed exterminator has sought for righteousness to prevail during the course of history. Harvest day in the Bible, or better known as judgment day, does not present a cruel, unjust God declaring the salvation of some and the destruction of others. No, the great harvester judges on the basis of the difference. Just as the farmer on the harvest day looked at one bundle and said it was wheat and the other bundle was tares, so will God judge people on the basis of what they are in character. If a person has chosen righteousness in Christ. God will vindicate this choice. If a person has chosen to live apart from God as an enemy, God will declare the person to be an enemy of unrighteousness.

Any picture of a cruel, tyrannical disposition in the almighty God at judgment day does not come from the Bible. No doubt our forefathers painted God's judgment in colors not creditable to the love of God seen in Jesus Christ.

It might come from human imagination, but, to be sure, this picture does not come from the Bible. There will be many surprises on judgment day, but it will be over who are God's people and who are not. No one will be surprised over God's action. His nature on harvest day will be what it has always been. He will judge on the actual difference which people have decided during their lifetime.

God will vindicate righteousness. Think about the nature of the farmer in the parable for a moment. Would he have been a good farmer if he allowed the tares to ruin the good crop? Or would the farmer have been a good farmer if the tares had prevailed rather than the wheat? The answers to the questions are obvious.

Now think about God. The Lord could eradicate evil at any time. He permits evil with the determination that righteousness will prevail during history. Ultimately God will terminate history and he will remove the presence of evil. We cannot conceive of God as permitting to wickedness a permanent place in his universe. A God tolerant of unholiness is a contradiction in terms.

The Bible pictures God as the one who will settle the ultimate issues of life. On one hand, God will arrange eternity for the righteous. These will hear the blessings of God, and they will enjoy fellowship with the Lord and with the redeemed. On the other hand, God will give the sentence of final exclusion from his presence to the unrighteousness. Alfred Lord Tennyson said:

> Hell? If the souls of men were immortal
> as men have been told,
> The lecher would cleave to his lusts, and the
> miser would yearn for his gold.
> And so there were Hell for ever! But were
> there a God as you say,
> His Love would have power over Hell till it
> utterly vanished away.

God will pronounce judgment upon those unrighteous, not

because love has no power, but because love will not violate their freedom. Hell represents God's vindication of the freedom of the human will.

The parable commonly known as the wheat and tares can be called a picture of the weed exterminator. Within the simple story is the truth that all of life, the history of the world, has its beginning and its end in God. All of us came from God. All of us have deserted him. The question is whether we are willing to be drawn again to God through Christ and to live with him. The course of history shows us the action of the enemy. But we get a picture of God who differentiates between righteousness and unrighteousness. The weed exterminator knows at this moment the destination. Someday he will make an ultimate separation. Whatever truths this parable teaches, it tells of a loving, righteous harvester who is willing to make anyone righteous.

10.
The Land Owner

Many years ago an ambitious man started a grocery business in a small building. He kept fresh meats and vegetables and a good stock of other groceries. He treated his customers kindly, giving them opportunities for bargains. Because of his good practices, the man's business grew. A larger building had to be secured. More employees had to be hired. He selected people to work in his stores who would be industrious. He rewarded them with good wages, fringe benefits, and good working conditions.

This man's grocery business grew in an unbelievable way. His store grew larger and larger. He then added new stores in various sections of the city, maintaining the same practices to his employees and to his customers. Now this person has numerous grocery stores scattered throughout a large city. In every grocery store there is a large photograph of the founder and owner of this large grocery chain.

Many businesses and corporations hang a picture of the founder and owner in a conspicuous place. It reminds the employees of the person who gave them the opportunity to work.

Have you ever thought that in the Bible there are numerous pictures of God as the owner of mankind. A. M. Hunter in the book *The Parables Then and Now* calls the story of the parable about work and wages recorded in Matthew 20:1–16, the parable of "The Good Employer." [1] The portrait of God as employer appears early in Genesis when he is portrayed as the founder of the company. God got the cosmos started, and he keeps it going. The word did not originate without a cause. God is the founder of the cosmos. William Harbert Carruth described it:

> A fire-mist and a planet—
>   A crystal and a cell
> A jelly-fish and a saurian,
>   And caves where the cave-men dwell;
> Then a sense of law and beauty
>   And a face turned from the clod,—
> Some call it Evolution,
> And others call it God.

The Bible portrays God as the president and founder of the cosmos.

As one looks through the picture album you can see the disclosure of God as a good employer who still runs the cosmos. He did not create the universe and human beings and leave the world in complete rule of others. God's competitor (Satan) sought to take over his business, but God still holds the control. Employees with arrogant pride and false wisdom think they know more than the boss. Consequently they seek to run the universe according to the way they desire. But God still retains control of the cosmos. He has not lost it to the competitor or to the bad employees. God still rules the universe and the affairs of human destiny.

Jesus frequently used pictures of a land owner to describe God's ways. He also compared the Lord with a householder who entrusted servants with responsibilities (Luke 12:42–48). He told about a servant responsible for managing the master's estate (Luke 16:1–13). These and other parables describe God as the land owner or the good employer. One of the most prominent pictures is the one in Matthew 20:1–16. Let us look at the story to get this picture of God. It was autumn in Palestine, and the grape harvest was at hand.

So a land owner went out early one morning to engage harvesters. At six o'clock he found some idle men in the marketplace and agreed to pay them a denar for a day's work. This group went to work immediately. Then at nine o'clock the employer found some other people idle in the marketplace. He asked them to join the other workers and told them he would pay what was right. So they went to work. At noon and again at three o'clock, he did likewise. Then, at five o'clock he found some more idle workers. He asked them to join the other workers in the vineyard.

An hour later the surprise came when the employer paid the workers. The latecomers were paid first. Though they were entitled to approximately eight pence, each one received a denar, a full day's wage. The first group, who worked all day long, looked at the transaction and protested. They said, "These workers worked only one hour, and yet you gave them the same amount as those who worked twelve hours. Is that just?" The employer said, "Look! I agreed to pay you a denar a day. You went to work with that agreement. Now I have given you your denar. Are you jealous because I am kind to the others?"

This simple story paints a portrait of God. It does not give a lesson in economics, but it gives theological glimpses of God. The workers related to a benevolent land owner who graciously selected them to work. He expected each worker to be diligent. In his settlement he was fair. The parable gives a portrait of a good employer.

Gracious in Selection

A casual reading of the parable of the good employer might cause one to see the wrong picture of God. When I first read the parable, I thought badly of the owner. It didn't seem fair to pay the workers who worked all day the same wages as those who only worked an hour. But a closer reading of the parable yielded the conclusion that Jesus was not talking about equal pay for equal work. He was not talking about economics but theology. The parable gives us the picture of a God gracious in his selection of people. God is like the employer in the story. The employer of the story demonstrates a gracious attitude and action.

God selects people without any basis of merit. Usually employers select people on the basis of qualification. The workers hired at six, nine, noon, three, and five o'clock were selected without any distinction.

Neither here nor anywhere else was our Lord speaking in matters of economics. One has to be careful not to glean industrial ideas from the story. It is surely impossible to read this story without seeing that the heart of the teller is moved at the spectacle of unemployment. He is compassionate over the men standing idle in the marketplace. The employer knew the plight of the unemployed, therefore he selected workers on basis of plight rather than the basis of merits. God, the good employer, selects people who are caught in the tragic plight of God. He reacts and responds with graciousness to them.

An amazing trait of God is that he makes no distinction. Probably the whole story grew out of Jesus' answering his critics the Pharisees. These Jews imagined their piety entitled them to a special claim on God's reward. They complained that Jesus opened the doors of the kingdom to all the undesirable characters of Palestine. When Jesus told about graciousness without distinction, he illustrated the truth about the grace of God. It means that no matter what a person's status is in life, he is equally dear to God. In the picture of God one cannot derive the idea that there is a favored nation or a favored person with God.

Discard any pictures of God which you might have that portray him as one who has favorites. We still have people who suppose their piety gives them a special claim on God's favor. Men of God have caught a glimpse of God's grace and preached about a God who would receive without distinction. John Wesley took the gospel to the people of his day, colliers, weavers, day laborers. William Booth offered "soup, soap, and salvation" to the East-enders of London. Anyone who creates a picture of God from a few select looks at a human caricature and not a biblical portrait does not see a true portrait of God.

God selects people for the purpose of doing good to them. The employer went to the marketplace. These men who gathered in the marketplace looked for work. The marketplace resembled the unemployment office in America. A person would go there and wait to be hired for work. The employer came to the market place and saw these people needing work. They were willing to work for a denar.

When the employer hired these people in the marketplace he did them a favor. Not only did he give them the opportunity to work, but he also gave them wages. This gives us a picture of an employer who desired to give good things—to seek after the best interests—of those in the marketplace.

What a great picture of God's grace! The traditional definition of God's grace is "the unmerited favor of God." One of my seminary professors told us a more workable idea about God's grace. He said, "The grace of God is all that God has done for mankind to make him better." All that God gives is of grace. We cannot earn what God gives us. We cannot deserve any of God's favors. What God does for us is done out of the goodness of his heart. It is not a reward. It is grace.

God bestowed his favor upon human beings with the creation of the world. With the giving of the law he revealed his graciousness. God's gracious nature and essence is the basis for his gifts to man in Jesus Christ (cf. Eph. 1:6; 2:8–9). Grace is the motive of redemption (2 Cor. 8:9). By grace through a person's faith one is justified (Rom. 3:24). In the knowledge of his grace we wait for the consummation of our salvation and appearing of our Lord Jesus Christ (Titus 2:11–13).

The parable of the good employer makes the grace of God explicitly clear. It reminds us that God does not deal with us on a basis of merits. God accepts us irrespective of who we might be and then bestows undeserved favors upon us.

Firm in Expectation

The owner of the vineyard was a good employer. He gave diligence to the harvest of his grapes. Furthermore, he sought to help the laborers. No employer deserves the description "good" who does not look out for the good of the business and for the betterment of the employees. You can not respect an employer who does not take an interest in the business. Employees will not respect an employer who allows workers to do as they please. Though workers might want to sit and do nothing, they would not respect an employer who was not somewhat firm in his expectations.

You can respect God, the good employer. He is firm in his expectations. The householder expected people to work. He did not want them to be idle. In other New Testament snapshots where God is presented as a householder, land-owner, or some other type of employer, the picture always depicts one firm in expectation. Jesus told a story about a nobleman who was to go on a journey. Before he left, he called in his ten servants and entrusted them with responsi-bilities. He said, "Occupy till I come" (Luke 19:13, cf. Luke 11:11–27). In another story, Jesus told of an employer who entrusted his employees (servants) with differing talents—to one he gave five, to another two, and to another one. The point of the story was that the employer strongly expected the servants to be faithful and to be diligent with their respective talents. To the diligent, the Lord said, "Well done, thou good and faithful servant" (Matt. 25:21). In no place in the New Testament is God pictured as a tolerant, easygoing employer who allows his employees to do as they please. He is firm in his expectations.

God is firm in his expectation because of the importance of the work. The parable of the good employer depicted a scene common toward the end of September. The grapes ripened at this time. In October the early rains would begin. If the grapes were not harvested before the rains fell, they would be ruined. To get the grapes harvested meant a frantic race against time. The employer wanted to get whoever he could for whatever time they could work. He searched for laborers for the good of the grape harvest. He demanded diligence in labor because of the importance of the grape harvest. This vineyard owner would not have deserved the title "good employer" if he did not consider the good of the business.

How much more important is the work of God! God takes a special interest in bringing rebellious human beings back into a relationship with him, with themselves, and with fellow human beings. You might call God's business a restoration process which leads to a beautiful life. No business is more important than a happy fellowship with the Creator. No business is more serious than working for wholeness of being. No business is more profitable than one which seeks to create a Christian, interpersonal relationship. It is no wonder that God is so firm in his expectations.

God does not tolerate laziness or disobedience from his employees. God's business is important and it demands diligence and obedience. No business can survive with lazy, inactive workers. Moreover, a business is in deep trouble when employees are not loyal to the desires, wishes, and regulations of the employer. Consequently, God is a good employer. He demands diligence for his workmen. He demands absolute obedience and allegiance.

God is firm in his expectations because of the good of the employees. The vineyard owner employed the laborers and demanded diligence because of their good. Getting to work put food on the tables of the worker's family. Obeying the demands of the owner developed the personal lives of the workmen. A good employer is not one who demands much from the laborers for his selfish interest. Instead, the employer is firm in expectation because of what it does to the laborer.

My first employer was my father. He paid me in the summer to work in his automobile parts store. What a demanding person he was! He expected me to arrive at work on time, preferably before time. He demanded that I stay until closing time. During the day, he demanded that I wait on the customers with courtesy. He required me to keep the store clean, to replenish the shelves, to make necessary deliveries, and to do any other job that was necessary.

Oftentimes, I thought my father's firm expectations were too rigid and severe, especially when he would not deviate for times of recreation. But looking back on that experience, I feel that my father was a good employer. His demands taught me many lessons of life. His firm employment taught me such things as disciplined living with time, courteous treatment of others, cleanliness of appearance, and learning the necessity of work. The firmness of his expectations was to benefit me, not to display his pecularities.

God is firm in his expectations because of the good it brings to us. We can worship and adore a good employer who demands diligence. We know that every demand which he makes on our life is an attemtpt to make us into our authentic and intended self.

Just in Settlement

Now let us look closer into the employer's settlement with the laborers. The vineyard owner found some potential workmen standing idle in the marketplace at six o'clock. He agreed to pay them a denar a day. They understood that they were to work the entire day, and they were satisfied with the salary. At nine o'clock the employer hired some other idle workers and promised to pay them "a fair wage." They went to work content that the employer would be just in his settlement. The employer hired other workers at twelve and three o'clock and promised to pay them a "fair wage." Then, at about five o'clock, an hour before sunset, the owner met more unemployed workers, and he hired them for a "fair wage."

The surprise comes in the settlement. Jewish law required an employer not to "keep back man's wages till next morning" (Lev. 19:13). The employer was a true person to the law, so he called the workers together and paid them, beginning with the last ones hired and working to the first ones hired. When the first ones employed saw the late arrivals get a denar, they protested. They thought the employer was unjust.

Nothing in the story suggests an unjust employer. Read the story closely and you will conclude that he was fair in his settlement. Of course you need to know that Jesus told the story to answer the Pharisees. These were the people who thought they had a special claim on God's reward. They complained when Jesus opened himself to undesirable characters. This story is not intended to be a disclosure of fair labor practices. It is the picture of God as a good employer, who hires self-righteous, snobbish Pharisees and also undesirable publicans and sinners into his vineyard. This tells us some great truths about God's fair treatment of people.

God's settlement is according to his sovereignty. Each group of laborers in the parable needed to recognize that the owner was the boss. It was neither their privilege nor their responsibility to run the vineyard. They were not allowed to set the practices of hiring, firing, or settlement. They were the laborers, and they were to be subservient to the owner's sovereignty. The employer hired the workers for a day's pay, a fair and just wage. He hired the others for a "fair price." If he wanted to give them a day's pay, this was his privilege. He owned the business, and he could do as he pleased.

God is the sole and sovereign employer. He makes the rules. He gives the worker's compensation. He exacts the settlement. He can do as he pleases. He is the sovereign Lord. But as we look into the way God handles the business of the universe and life, he always does what is right. In no way does the sovereignty of God picture anything about God but fairness.

One of man's biggest mistakes is to picture God as one of the employees and not the boss. God rules by virtue of his creation of the universe. He is the only God, and he rules supreme. "Sing praises to God, sing praises: Sing praises unto our King, sing praises. For God is the King of all the earth: sing ye praises with understanding. God reigneth over the heathen: God sitteth upon the throne of his holiness" (Ps. 47:6–8). There is only one God, who is supreme, absolute, and authoritative. Man must look upon him as the sole and sovereign employer. All peoples of the earth are subject to his sovereign rule. Because God is the boss, he can do as he pleases.

God's settlement is according to his grace. Each group of laborers did not do the same work, but they did receive the same pay. Again let us remember that this is not a proposal for economic settlement. This is a picture of a good employer, just and fair in his settlement with laborers. The men who worked all day were not defrauded. They received a generous wage in fulfillment of a just promise. But when the men who had worked only one hour received as much as they, they murmured.

The prominent truth of this parable is that God deals and settles with human beings according to grace and not merit. The later workers probably did not deserve the generosity, but the employer gave it to them. Actually the generosity of the employer motivated him to get the six o'clock workers. He dealt in grace, and he settled the day's work with grace.

God settles accounts with people according to grace, not merit. There is no way to explain the transition of payment when the employer gave each laborer the pay. The grace of God defies analysis. It is beyond the scope of human definition. God settles with every one of us out of the goodness of his heart. No one gets what they deserve. They receive infinitely more. God does not settle his accounts on the basis of a person's merits, but on the basis of his grace. How fortunate it is that God does not deal with us on the basis of justice. God's settlement issues out of love. There is no way that finite employees can understand the fabulous greatness of the great employer.

11.
The King of Kings

In 1922 Howard Carter, a British archaeologist, and his patron, Lord Carnarvon, discovered the tomb of the ancient Eygptian boy-king named Tutankhamen. Thousands of objects were removed from the tomb's four chambers. Tutankhamen, or commonly known as "King Tut," ruled Egypt from 1334 to 1325 B.C. and amassed treasures of enormous value. The treasures contained the solid gold mask of King Tut and the wooden gilt statuette of the protective goddess Selket. King Tut became well known because of his wealthy rule. The contents of his tomb added greatly to the knowledge of Egyptian civilization.

The Egyptian government made an unprecedented loan of the treasure of King Tut to the United States. These treasures were displayed from September of 1977 to January of 1978. They were displayed in New Orleans, Los Angeles, New York, Chicago, Seattle, and Washington, D.C. In all four cities the initial response was overwhelming. While observing these ornate treasures, I marveled at the fame and wealth of King Tut. Yet, while observing these treasures, I thought of another king. The King of kings. It is none other than the Lord himself.

One of the prominent portraits of God throughout the Bible is of a king. In the Old Testament there is no commoner title for God than king. "The Lord is king for ever and ever" (Ps. 10:16). He is the "king of glory" (Ps. 24:7–10). "He is the king of all the earth" (Ps. 47:7). "The Holy One of Israel

110

is our king" (Ps. 89:18).

Looking through the New Testament yields many places where God is portrayed as a king. From the beginning to the end, Jesus explained God in terms of a king. The wise men came to visit the Christ child with the question, "Where is he that is born king of the Jews?" (Matt. 2:2). The angelic messengers announced to Mary about her son: "The Lord shall give unto him the throne of his father David: And he shall reign over the house of Jacob for ever" (Luke 1:32–33). During Jesus' preaching and teaching the essence of his message was about a kingdom. When Jesus entered Jerusalem for the last time, he presented himself as a king riding on a donkey. When the Lord was on the cross, he was portrayed as a king. The penitent thief asked him, "Lord, remember me when thou comest into thy kingdom" (Luke 23:42). The early church frequently gave the picture of God as the king. "Who is the blessed and only Potentate, the King of kings, and Lord of lords" (1 Tim. 6:15). Other rulers such as Pharaohs, Caesars, and presidents may have the name ruler, but only God is the King of kings. The title "King of kings and Lord of Lords" is attributed to Christ in Revelation 19:16. No greater portrait of God can be seen in the Bible than the fact that God is the emperor, king, Pharaoh, president, or czar of all and for all ages.

Qualified in Character

To be an effective king one must possess something more than popularity or power. The great kings and the great rulers over nations and the affairs of mankind have been those of unusual character. The American government has been careful in recent years to investigate the character of those elected to serve them.

Jesus portrayed God as the eminently qualified king. He is without flaw in character. The senate and the Central Intelligence Agency could look closely into the character of the

King of kings. He could withstand close investigation and emerge from the studies as the perfect God without a flaw of character. The greatness of the King of kings must be seen in character.

God's character involves holiness. Isaiah, saw the portrait of God as a king. "In the year that King Uzziah died I saw also the Lord sitting upon a throne, high and lifted up, and his train filled the temple. Above it stood the seraphim . . . And one cried unto another and said, Holy, holy, holy, is the Lord of hosts: the whole earth is full of his glory. And the posts of the door moved at the voice of him that cried, and the house was filled with smoke. Then said I, Woe is me! for I am undone; because I am a man of unclean lips, and I dwell in the midst of a people of unclean lips: for mine eyes have seen the King, the Lord of hosts" (Isa. 6:1–5). Isaiah saw a glimpse of God as a king more majestic and more powerful than any king before or since. Isaiah learned of the holy character of God.

The holiness of God suggests God's uniqueness. God is unique in that no one else could be compared to God. He is "wholly other" in his person. Furthermore, God is morally pure in his relations with others. Isaiah became aware that the portrait of God as king portrayed God as infinitely transcending human beings with regard to goodness. Something in Isaiah's vision of God caused him to see his own sinfulness and the sinfulness of the people in whose presence he lived. The King of kings is pure, separate, and moral. He is qualified to be king.

God's character includes righteousness. This means that God's character is upright. In him is no taint of evil. John said, "God is light, and in him is no darkness at all" (1 John 1:5). Whatever else John meant to say about God, he communicated the absolute purity of God's character. He is free from any evil tendency.

The righteousness of God also describes how God acts

toward people. In all of God's relations with humankind the righteous God acts justly. Because God is righteous in character, his treatment of others will be just. God's righteousness means that God will stand for the right as opposed to the wrong, the pure as opposed to the impure.

God's character involves love. God is a mighty king who treats his subjects with love. Many rulers have abused, oppressed, or manipulated their subjects. But God displays himself with a character of love. Love is the nature of God. John said, "God is love" (1 John 4:8). This helps us to understand that everything God does is an act of love. There is nothing that God does that is inconsistent with love. Love is the motive in all that he does. He created because he loved. He preserves, guides and redeems because God's nature is to love.

God's character was clearly demonstrated in the life and ministry of Jesus. If you want to see a flesh and blood demonstration of holiness, righteousness, and love, you can look at Jesus. Jesus was the exhibition of God's character to the world. In Jesus Christ, the abstract terms of God's character became knowable and visible. God's character cannot be strange to us. Jesus manifested the nature of the heavenly Father. Without a doubt, God deserves the title King of kings.

Capable in Leadership

Rulers must not only possess character, but they must possess the ability to govern people. As you read about the great rulers of history, you will discover their unusual skills in leading people. Some rulers have been good people, but they did not possess the skills capable of directing the affairs of a nation.

Superlatives are not adequate to describe the Lord's leadership. Compared to the ability of his majesty and skill all other kings are only a match vainly endeavoring to illuminate the world. Shelley, in one of his sonnets, writes of meeting a traveler from Egypt. The traveler had found in Egypt the remains of a statue, with two trunkless legs, and near them a broken face. On the pedestal was the inscription:

> My name is Ozymandias, king of kings:
> Look on my works, ye Mighty, and despair!

Ozymandias had the audacity to call himself the "king of kings." He left behind only a couple of legs and a broken visage in stone. Jesus deserves the title King of kings, for he inaugurated and left an eternal kingdom. No one possesses the unusual skill of God to rule the lives of people.

The great manifestation of God as a king can be seen in the life and ministry of Jesus. People recognized in Jesus the qualities of a king. Nathaniel said: "Rabbi, thou art the Son of God; thou art the king of Israel!" (John 1:49). Jesus did not manipulate people to gain followers. He called them. He taught them so they might lead others. He lived an exemplary life before them and inspired daring dedication. In every sense of the word, Jesus demonstrated the supreme capabilities of a leader. He deserves the title King of kings.

Let us look more specifically into the way God rules. Jesus revealed that God demands absolute allegiance. In leading the disciples he demanded that they have absolute loyalty to him. Throughout Israel's history God demanded an undivided loyalty to him. Israel was never a strong and influential nation while possessing a dual loyalty. They had to worship and serve God alone. The first four commandments in the Decalogue specify the matter of allegiance to God: no other gods; not things, but God: respect for God: and reverence for God's day. The Ten Commandments begin by laying down one's duty to God. This means that God demands first place.

When Jesus taught about the kingdom, he specifically mentioned the preeminence of putting the Lord first. The

Sermon on the Mount begins with the admission that we cannot live life by ourselves. We need God's help. Jesus taught in praying that God's name must be held in reverence. This means to place God in the uniquely supreme place and obey him. Then Jesus said to pray, "Thy kingdom come. Thy will be done in earth, as it is in heaven" (Matt. 6:10). This is a parallelism. The second half of the statement explains, amplifies, and develops the first. So we get an idea of the way Jesus rules. He demands those in the kingdom of God to obey the Father's will as perfectly on earth as it is in heaven.

No earthly kingdom can survive with divided loyalties. Rulers realize that subjects within nations must exercise respect and loyalty to those who rule. Empires have fallen because people lost respect for rulers. Kings, potentates, czars, Pharaohs, and presidents have used ridiculous measures to solidify allegiance to the state. God knows how to lead. He demands absolute allegiance to him. Those who submit to the Lord discover that he is worthy of our worship and allegiance.

Let us look deeper into another way that God leads. He also leads by demanding proper association with other people. When Jesus related to the disciples, he taught them principles of proper relationships with other people. God reveals himself to us that we may relate properly to people around us.

During Israel's history, God gave six commandments in the Decalogue which describe his technique of relating to others. After a proper relationship of absolute reverence for the Lord, God gave six principles of duty to others. He tells us to honor our fathers and mothers. The home is the pivotal point of building relationships with people. It is within the home that formative character traits develop. One learns, or fails to learn, how to live harmoniously within society and to respond creatively to his environment. The other five commandments might be obeyed more easily if we obeyed the first four and the fifth. Nonetheless, God commanded Israel to hold in high regard the sacredness of life; to be faithful in marriage; to respect the property of another, to be truthful, and to guard inward desires. What a way to run a kingdom! No wonder God can be considered the King of kings!

Jesus Christ manifested the techniques of God's rule. People had heard of God's method of rule from the law, but Jesus gave dramatic visibility to his method during his earthly life and ministry. Jesus went to the heart of the matter about relating to others. Jesus tracks the beginning of relationship to the heart of a person. The person in right relationship with God can relate to others.

Supreme in Lordship

Earthly kings may possess unusual character and powerful qualities of leadership, but Jesus possesses a quality no other ruler can have. He is absolutely supreme in lordship. There is a "differentness" in God's kingdom and the rulers of the world. Earthly rulers come and go. They have their time on the stage of history, but it is a limited time.

I saw the Conquerors riding by
With cruel lips and faces wan:
Musing on kingdoms sacked and burned,
There rode the Mongol, Genghis Khan.

And Alexander, like a god,
Who sought to weld the world in one:
And Caesar with his laurel wreath:
And like a thing from Hell, the Hun;

And leading, like a star the van,
Heedless of outstretched arm and groan,

> Inscrutable Napoleon went
> Dreaming of empire, and alone . . .
>
> They all perished from the earth,
> As fleeting shadows from a glass,
> And, conquering down the centuries
> Came Christ, the Swordless, on an ass.

God rules in history. Some may think that God is going to rule someday. Jesus never gave this impression. He communicated that God is on the throne ruling and reigning now. There has never been a time when God lost the sovereign control of history. God has always been in control.

In the life and ministry of Jesus Christ, God gave the world a beautiful picture that he still controls history. In Jesus we see the execution of the kingdom. He perfectly obeyed the will of the Father. He fulfilled the Lord's techniques and commandments. He obeyed God and served human beings all the days of his life.

During Jesus' lifetime, enemies threatened his life and belittled his ministry. But Jesus withstood all of the assaults and defeated every enemy. When human beings crucified the Lord, it seemed that God died. Some contemporary theologians wrote the obituary of God, dating his death the crucifixion of Jesus. People around the world thought the King of kings had put down his crown, laid aside his kingdom, and passed into oblivion.

Believing these facts about the King neglects the King's history. Three days after the King was buried, he arose from the grave. The resurrection tells us something about how powerful the King rules in history. Within history and in human flesh God defeated life's greatest enemy, namely death, and declares emphatically, "I am the sovereign King of kings." The King of kings rose from death proving that God governs the world, declaring that God is stronger than evil, and that God's life is stronger than death. Jesus demonstrated dramatically that nothing or no one can defeat God.

God is ruling today. The passing of years has not threatened his reign. The King of kings reigns today in the affairs of men.

In one of his plays John Masefield tells how Pilate's wife was anxious to know what had happened to Jesus. Her name was Procula. She sent for Longinus, the centurion who had been in charge of the crucifixion. Longinus told Procula that he died on the cross. "So you think," said Procula, "that he is finished and his work is ended?" "No, madam," said Longinus, "I do not." "What then?" said Procula. And Longinus answered, "He is set free throughout the world where neither Jew nor Greek can stop his truth." When Jesus died on the cross and rose from the dead, he was set free to reign in the lives of people around the world.

God rules beyond history. Earthly kings can rule in a time span. They can conquer, lead, and execute the affairs of a state. But Jesus leads beyond history. God has the power to stop time and rule in absolute sovereignty. God will ultimately rule the world. Before him every knee will bow, and every tongue will confess that he is Lord.

Jesus revealed that the world is on its way to a final goal when the kingdoms of the world shall be the kingdoms of the Lord. This will happen when the King of kings returns to earth. It is useless to speculate about the exact time of the coronation day, but we can still sing "The King Is Coming." We can make the necessary preparations.

The writer of the Revelation caught a grand glimpse of God. Some think that the writer only saw a vision of life beyond history. Others think that he saw a vision of the sovereignty of God over the affairs in history and a vision of the triumphant King beyond history. All interpreters of the Revelation would agree that the King of kings will reign when time ends. "And he hath on his vesture and on his thigh a name written, KING OF KINGS, AND LORD OF LORDS" (Rev. 19:16). This describes what God is— conquering King, righteous King, King of kings. This means that God is sovereign and supreme over all rulers of the earth.

Several years ago I visited the majestic Westminster Abbey. In a part of this place is a spot known as St. Edwards' Chapel. There one of England's most precious relics can be observed, the ancient Coronation Chair. Every coronation of the king of England has used that chair since Edward I in the 1300's. While looking on that unusual throne, I got a glimpse of another throne. This is God's throne where all the illustrious kings, queens, Pharaohs, czars, presidents, and potentates must bow ultimately.

Nothing teaches any more about God than a glimpse of God as the King of kings. Jesus announced the Kingdom and explained the king. He persuaded people to respond to the loving king and to enthrone God as king within their hearts.

12.
The Exorcist

In May of 1971, William P. Blatty's book *The Exorcist* appeared. Because of its popularity, it went into numerous printings. The story was made into a motion picture, and millions of Americans stood in line at theaters to view the film. Blatty's story was the discussion of television and radio. Prime time was given to *The Exorcist*. It was the main topic of discussion in newspapers and magazines. Theologians said that during this time Americans suffered from an outbreak of "demonmania," which means a fascination with demons.

Let us review the story of this unusual book and the film based on it. The story takes place around Washington D.C., near the Georgetown University campus. In the story there is an actress making a film on the campus. She lived with her twelve-year-old daughter. As the story unfolds, the young daughter began to have some unusual symptoms. She had been playing with a Ouija board. In the large house the mother and daughter rented, unusual events began to happen. The young girl was awakened in the middle of the night by weird movements of her bed. The mother heard strange sounds in the attic. The story deepened progressively. Finally the daughter was assumed to be physically ill. Numerous physicians examined her for brain damage, or some other physical causes for her strange and unusual symptoms. They could find nothing wrong. Psychiatrists were then called to give a battery of tests. Nothing showed up of any basic psychological problem. In the meantime, her symptoms worsened with contorted facial features and other actions not typical of a twelve-year-old girl.

Two Roman Catholic priests appeared in the story. The older priest had just returned from the Middle East. The younger priest combined the use of psychiatry with the Roman Church's ancient practice of exorcism.

The demons seemed to take stronger possession of the young girl. Under the demoniac influence, she killed a man who came to her mother's house. The mother was distraught. Finally, she sought the help of the two priests. They tried to determine if the girl's case were one of demon possession. They soon decided it was, and they gave her the rite of exorcism. The story concluded with the elder priest dying of a heart attack. The young priest in frustration and rage invited the demon into himself. He hurled himself from the window and was killed. Just before his death he received the last rite of the Roman Catholic Church, and thereby found himself having overcome the force of evil.

William Blatty wrote an interesting and unparalleled money-making story. The movie producers did an outstanding job with his story, following closely the events creating horrifying and incredible sights for the viewer to behold, and producing sounds which would make the calm shiver. Thousands of readers of the novel and millions of viewers conjured up unusual ideas about God and his relationship to evil.

Unfortunately people look in the wrong places to find many of their beliefs about God and evil. William Blatty's novel *The Exorcist* does not give a biblical picture of God and his relationship to evil. The best portraits of God are found in the biblical framework and not in human projections. To get a genuine portrait of God, and his relationship to evil, look in the gospel narratives. The Gospel according to Mark contains numerous snapshots of Jesus dealing with demon possessed people. These miraculous accounts furnish us with the picture of God as the only exorcist. Only Jesus can defeat the Evil One. Let us look at these various snapshots in Mark and learn something about God's attitude and action toward evil.

God's Insight into Evil

Mark records numerous incidents where Jesus encountered people who had unclean spirits. The reality of the demoniac was acknowledged by the ancient world. The whole ancient world believed strongly in demons. Adolph Harnack says: "The whole world and the circumambient atmosphere were filled with devils; not merely idolatry, but every phase and form of life was ruled by them. They sat on thrones, hovered around cradles. The world was literally a hell." [1] Jesus demonstrated a marvelous insight into the evil powers.

God acknowledges the reality of evil in the world. Jesus viewed life as a real struggle between the power of evil and the power of God. He did not deal with demon-possessed people by analyzing every problem related to evil. Jesus acknowledged that an evil power threatened human beings, and he did not give lectures on the origin of evil. Someone put it this way—suppose a man wakes up to find his house on fire, he does not sit down in a chair and embark upon the reading of a treatise entitled "The Origin of Fires in Private Houses." He grabs every defense possible and deals with the fire. Jesus did not speculate about evil; he dealt with it and gave to others the power to overcome evil.

Strange as it may seem, some people feel compelled to describe the origin of evil. Usually these people are more concerned about giving a lecture on "The Origin of Evil in Today's Society" rather than fighting evil. In each of Jesus' encounters with evil recorded in Mark, there is not one attempt to explain about the demoniac powers. Instead, Jesus acknowledges that an intruder has come into the world where he does not belong.

God characterizes the nature of evil. Though God is not interested in telling the origin of evil, he gives amazing insight into the nature of evil. Jesus knows that a person is a total being. Therefore, Jesus was concerned with biological needs, psychological needs, and spiritual needs. When Jesus dealt with the demon-possessed people, he gave an insight into the nature of evil. Whenever a person was affected physically, psychologically, or spiritually, the New Testament world used the term "demon-possessed" or "evil spirit." These terms in Jesus' day could have described a physical, mental, or spiritual malady.

For example, look at the snapshot in Mark 1:23 of the man in the synagogue with an "unclean spirit." The man could have suffered from some severe emotional problem. Evidently, he did not pose the threat that the man in the country of the Gadarenes did. Then look at the case of the boy possessed with a "dumb spirit" in Mark 9. He frothed at the mouth, and he often fell uncontrolled into the fire. These symptoms bear all the resemblance to what we would call epilepsy in today's world. The first-century world labeled this as a "dumb spirit." There are some clear cases in the New Testament which cannot be explained either physically or psychologically. Clearly enough, these people allowed themselves to be influenced by the evil one. In the New Testament sense of the word one is possessed by the demoniac power when he or she gives over to it. This involves a gradual takeover of the life.

The Exorcist portrays one being possessed by the demoniac without choosing. The New Testament never characterizes evil in this manner. The basic theological premise of the Bible is the freedom of human beings. God would not allow evil to possess a person. God will not force himself upon a person. Therefore, he will not allow evil to intrude into a person's life without a choice.

God's Opposition of Evil

Wherever you see Jesus encounter evil, you see that he opposed evil. To the possessed man in the synagogue, Jesus said: "Hold thy peace, and come out of him" (Mark 1:25). On another occasion Jesus drove the demons which tortured the man from the country of the Gadarenes into some swine (Mark 5:1–17). A Syrophoenician woman sought the Master and asked him to cast the devil from her daughter. When the woman returned home, she discovered that the devil had left her daughter (Mark 7:26). To a boy possessed with the dumb and deaf spirit, Jesus said: "Thou dumb and deaf spirit, I charge thee, come out of him, and enter no more into him" (Mark 9:25).

Jesus opposed evil irrespective of what form it took. He sought to heal those beset with some physical malady; to deal with those plagued by some emotional disorder; and to break the tenacious hold which people had allowed Satan to take on them. God reacts against any problem which hinders a person from becoming his authentic and true self.

God possesses authority over evil. Jesus demonstrated a serene confidence in the presence of the demoniac powers. He was not disturbed over their violent opposition to the Master. These powers exerted great sway on a person and when people gave in to the demoniac power they exerted great influence. God revealed in Jesus Christ that he possessed authority over all the powers. Jesus commanded evil spirits to come out of people. He transferred demons from people to pigs. Whatever the Lord wanted to do with the demoniac world, he could do.

Joachim Jeremias, in his book *New Testament Theology: The Proclamation of Jesus*, says: "Jesus enters this world enslaved by Satan with the authority of God, not only to exercise mercy, but above all to join battle with evil." [2] The Gospel of Mark depicts Jesus' exorcisms as battles. He combated anything that sought to hurt humanity.

Only God possesses the authority to battle with evil. Trying to remove evil and fighting the evil one has characterized human history. Exorcism, or the process of trying to rid a person of evil, prevailed from earliest times. During Jesus' day the Jews believed that Solomon had received the act of exorcism. Josephus in his monumental work on the Jewish people, *The Antiquities of the Jews,* said that "God enabled Solomon to learn the arts valid against demons." Josephus also related how he saw a Jewish exorcist, called Eleazar exorcise a demon from a man. He put a root, entwined with a magical root, below the sufferer's nostrils. He then uttered numerous incantations and drew the demon out through the nostrils. Eleazar made some proof that the demon had been exorcised. He had set a basin of water a little distance away. He commanded the demon to upset the water as he went away. In due time, according to Josephus, the basin was upset.

Numerous people claimed to have power or authority over the demons. William Blatty's book revived interest in the ancient Roman rite of exorcism. Neo-Pentecostal churches openly practice the ritual of exorcism. I read in a preacher's book of how people cast out demons from other people. He tells how the male sufferer spoke to him in a female voice and threw himself on the floor. This was followed by writhings and groanings with the person in a state of semiconsciousness. The preacher commanded the demon to depart, and the demon left with violent force.

Regardless of what you may think of the rituals and weird experiences regarding exorcism, one must acknowledge that the Bible gives only one picture of the true exorcist. People can seek deliverance from the evils and sorrows in incantations and elaborate rituals, but there is revealed in Jesus the serene confidence of authority. The exorcisms of the Master points to the reality of God's presence in the world to oppose evil.

God opposes evil because it seeks to harm humanity and to prevent actualization of true personhood. Jesus exorcised the demon from the man in the synagogue because it prevented the man from worship. Jesus opposed the demons in the man from the Gadarenes because it prevented him from living life as a human being. Wherever Jesus opposed demons, he did so to help people and not to demonstrate his great authority.

The collective word for demons is *mazzikin*, which means "ones who do harm." The demons, in some cases, were referred to as beings who were out to oppose God and to work harm to people. God cannot be happy with man suffering from any kind of harm, whether physically, emotionally, or spiritually. Jesus came to earth to oppose demons, for he loved man and he wanted people to have the best possible type of life. In God's scale of values, nothing is so important as a human soul. Anything that seeks to destroy the worth and dignity of personhood God opposes. Jesus' life and ministry gave dramatic visibility to God's opposition to evil. God is opposed to blindness, sickness, paralysis, leprosy, and other physical maladies. God is opposed to emotional disorders such as fear, anxiety, loneliness, depression, and other such problems. God is opposed to a will open to Satan. The ministry of Jesus gave a sign that God opposed anything that worked to harm humanity.

God's Victory over Evil

Look again at each snapshot of Jesus' encounter with evil. Who won? The answer is obvious. Jesus encountered various types of possessed people. There was strong opposition from the demoniac world against the Master. Often the possessed person gave remarks in an attempt to ward Jesus away. The opposition then turned into violent attack with the demons commanding Jesus to be silent and to depart. In every case

Jesus emerged victorious. This gives us the insight that God is absolutely supreme over soul.

God won the victory over evil in Jesus Christ. Jesus told a parable of the defeat of a strong man. It is recorded in Mark 3:22–30. He said there is only one way for a strong man to be defeated, and that is for a stronger man to master him. "No man can enter into a strong man's house, and spoil his goods, except he will first bind the strong man; and then he will spoil his house" (Mark 3:27). Jesus claimed to have entered in Satan's domain. He demonstrated that he was stronger than Satan. The devil's citadel was breached, and the strong man was defeated by the victorious Christ. The proof that Jesus defeated Satan abounded. Sufferers were healed. The diseased were restored to health. The disturbed found a clamness. The demon-possessed found a deliverance.

Evil fought tenaciously against the Lord throughout Jesus' life and ministry. Satan attacked the Lord at a weak moment immediately after his baptism. The tempter presented some plausible and attractive proposals to the Lord. Jesus resisted and won the battle. But the opposer would not let Jesus rest. In every point of being human, Jesus was tempted. But in each case the Lord emerged victorious. The cross and resurrection spelled the final doom of Satan. From that time Satan's power has been a limited power. He is no longer the conquering power of darkness. He is the defeated enemy. The enemy has not yet died, but his power can never be the same again. Jesus helps others to win the victory which he himself won.

God defeated evil in Jesus' life and ministry, and God promises ultimately to conquer all forms of evil. The New Testament interprets history as being moved by God toward a goal. God intends to rid the world of everything that seeks to harm man. The ministry of Jesus furnishes a microcosm of the ultimate, completed kingdom. It will be a time when God will reign supremely. John caught a glimpse of the ultimate defeat of evil: "And God shall wipe away all tears from their eyes; and there shall be no more death, neither sorow, nor crying, neither shall there be any more pain: for the former things are passed away" (Rev. 21:4). At the end of history God will terminate an old order, one beset with sorrow, pain, and death. These problems will be absent from the new order. This is a description of God's original creation fully restored. That is the portrait of the real exorcist.

God's final victory over Satan started with the incarnation. It was substantiated by the cross. Also, in the history of God's people, one can see Christians having triumphed over evil by God's power. Satan has a limited amount of power. God has promised to destroy Satan completely. The final and complete elimination of evil is certain. In the Revelation, John tells of the punishment of Satan: "And the devil that deceived them was cast into the lake of fire and brimstone, where the beast and false prophet are, and shall be tormented day and night for ever and ever" (Rev. 20:10). The victory of God will be complete when every vestige of evil will be obliterated and every enemy of human beings will be destroyed.

When I was a boy, I read Franklin W. Dixon's works about the Hardy boys. In this series, Joe and Frank's father was a detective. Oftentimes the brothers would find out the case their father was working, and they would subtly try to find the criminal. Once I remember my interest in *The Secret of the Old Mill*. Frank and Joe were made prisoners in an old house by some crooks. As I read the story my excitement began to build. It became so intense that I would put the book down and walk away from it. But I had to return. Finally, I could stand the suspense no longer. I turned to the final chapter and read where Joe and Frank stood with their father at the old house. Then I returned to the suspense part. I could read with ease, for I had read the final chapter.

One does not have to be in suspense about the victor in the

struggle of good and evil. The last chapter of the Bible portrays the exorcist as having destroyed the enemies and as ruling supremely. God is the only exorcist. He can rule over the power of evil in the world today. Someday he will exorcise evil from the world and will establish an order free from sin and suffering.

13.
The Social Worker

Most graduate schools require various types of examinations. Many give the Graduate Record Examination to check on a person's general educational background. Most schools give a Proficiency English Examination to check on a person's skill in using the English language. Many graduate schools require a psychological examination like the PF-16, a test designed to measure sixteen qualities of a person's personality.

My entrance into the graduate school required these examinations in addition to one more. One school required me to take the Thematic Apperception Test. This was one of the most unusual tests I had ever taken. The test has a series of pictures. The applicant has a private interview with a skilled counselor going through pictures with the applicant telling a story which you think the picture tells. The test supposedly reveals many facets about your inner feelings.

At times I have given a "Theological Apperception Test." In various groups and with different individuals I have asked them to tell me what kind of picture of God they have. Answers to this question have been interesting: "God is a mighty king ruling his subjects with love." "God is a righteous judge whose judgments are tempered by mercy." "God is like a gentle shepherd seeking the lost." "God in the New Testament is a mighty Redeemer." "I can see God in the New Testament as the loving Father." These and other answers have been given as people perceive of God when they read their Bible.

Once I gave my theological apperception test to a colleague. I asked one of my fellow professors "Ann, how do you picture God?" Her answer came back quickly and positively. "I think of God as the social worker." Then she said, "Look at the picture of the wounded traveler on the Jericho road. The good Samaritan helped this person." Later she quoted a familiar Scripture, "For I was an hungred, and ye gave me meat: I was thirsty, and ye gave me drink: I was a stranger, and ye took me in: Naked, and ye clothed me: . . . I was in prison, and ye came unto me" (Matt. 25:35–36). This person gave me one of the most interesting insights about God. She caused me to see something about God that I had never seen before. God as portrayed in the New Testament could be called the social worker.

Having this insight of God caused me to probe and to study about social work. In perhaps the leading textbook used for the subject I read: "Social work is the art and science of providing services designed to enhance the interpersonal competence and social functioning of people, both as individuals and in groups." [1] Judging by that definition and by a close reading of the New Testament, God could be seen as the social worker. He has always acted to provide a ministry which would enhance a person's competence and ability to function in society.

Let us look quickly through the gospel narratives and see how prominent the picture is of Jesus the social worker. Let us start with Jesus' preaching. He preached in the synagogue in Nazareth using Isaiah 61. The Lord announced that he was the bearer of good news for the dispossessed, the afflicted, and the oppressed. In the Lord's preaching he emphasizes social work. Stop and listen to a summarization of the Lord's ministry to the disciples of John the Baptist. "The blind receive their sight, and the lame walk, the lepers are cleansed, and the deaf hear, and the dead are raised up, and the poor have the gospel preached to them" (Matt. 11:5). Look at how Jesus spent his days during his ministry. He took time to care for physical, spiritual, emotional, and mental needs. Jesus dealt with such social matters as family, business, and government. Unquestionably God is portrayed in the New Testament as the social worker, seeking the betterment of an individual so that the person may relate more effectively in society. As we read through the New Testament we can see the qualities of the social worker.

The Capacity to Feel

Social workers must have the capacity to feel for the needs of people. One cannot help people without a genuine belief in the individual's worth and dignity. Moreover, a social worker needs to be gifted with the qualities of compassion, sympathy, and a great desire to help people. One cannot be a good social worker without deep feeling for the needy. For example, one cannot work with the aged without a gifted feeling for the older person. The best social workers are those who feel and relate positively to the people of particular plights.

Jesus portrayed the nature of God as one capable of feeling for a human being. God made human beings and he knows their inner makeup. He possesses the amazing capacity to feel for persons as no one else can feel. He is supreme in his heaven and he is present in human history knowing and understanding the problems of human beings. To think of God as "up yonder" and one who cannot understand is to get an image of God that the New Testament does not portray.

God has the capacity to feel the plight of people. One of the great snapshots that Jesus gave of God's attitude was his inner attitude toward a group of people. "When he saw the multitudes, he was moved with compassion on them, because they fainted and were scattered abroad, as sheep having no shepherd" (Matt. 9:36). The word translated compassion is *spagchnistheis* which is the strongest Greek word for pity. It describes the pity which moves a person to the depths of his being. In most cases, the word is used in reference to Jesus' compassion. As we study the New Testament we can see what moved the Master. He had pity for the sick and those in the grips of demoniac power. Our Lord was moved with compassion for other people's sorrow and hardship. The sight of the widow at Nain following the body of her son to burial moved his heart. Seeing hungry people moved the Master. He called upon his powers to feed the multitude. The Lord felt for lonely lepers. The sight of banished lepers called forth his pity and his power to heal. Furthermore, the Lord was moved to compassion by the world's meaningless meanderings.

The Lord must be deeply moved over world conditions' today. Let us never get the picture of a disgusted God or a despairing Lord. Let us always see that God looks upon a world with a compassion from the depths of his being. Think about how much God cares for world hunger. Think about how much the Lord cares for the diseased, the sick, and the handicapped. Imagine how much compassion God feels for those with mental illness and those beset with demoniac selfishness. Without a doubt the deepest pity of our Lord goes to those who exist without a meaning and a purpose for life. Immeasurable multitudes live out life wearied by a journey which seems to have no purpose or meaning. Some of the contemporary literature reflects the aimlessness of our present age: T. S. Eliot's *The Waste Land*, William Faulkner's *Sound and Fury*, Jean-Paul Sartre's *No Exit*, Albert Camus' *The Plague*, and Eugene O'Neill's *Long Day's Journey into Night*. Jesus feels deeply for man's alienation and isolation.

Jesus possessed the capacity to feel, for he took upon himself humanity. "For we have not an high priest which cannot be touched with the feelings of our infirmities; but was in all points tempted like as we are, yet without sin" (Heb. 4:15). Jesus has the capacity to feel because he went through everything a human being experiences. Some people often think of God the way ancient Greeks did. The Stoics, the highest Greek thinkers, said the primary attribute of God is *apatheia*. This means the essential inability to feel anything at all. The Greeks contended that God was beyond all feeling. The Epicureans conceived of their gods dwelling in the *intermundia*, the spaces between the world. There the gods were in complete detachment from the world. They were not even aware of it.

The New Testament brought a revolutionary picture of the true and living God. God feels for humans because he came to earth in human flesh and experienced everything a person must go through. Because God has known our life he can sympathize with the human plight.

' God has the capacity to feel because he believes in the potential of people. People enter into the field of social work believing that others can be better. Jesus never lost sight that every human being had marvelous potential. Jesus looked at Zacchaeus and believed in him. One would not have predicted that Zacchaeus could have changed. His encounter with the social worker caused him to give half of his goods to the poor.

The woman taken in adultery had little potential in the eyes of the community. One day she was caught in the act of adultery. Her accusers dragged her in the streets to stone her. The only potential they saw in her was disposal. But Jesus stooped and wrote in the sand. Her accusers disappeared. Jesus looked deeper than any person ever looked and saw potential. She became a new person and a faithful disciple.

No person can be an effective social worker with feelings that needy persons are nuisances and the best potential for them is death. God looks at everyone and says, "You have potential. You can be more than you are." With this understanding of a person's plight and with this optimistic belief in a person's betterment, Jesus is the best social worker. He has the capacity to feel.

The Technique to Help

Capable social workers have the skill and technique to help needy people. One cannot help others in need with well-wishing words. It takes a technique to help. Social workers employ various methods. They use casework. This is a method of helping people individually. It combines psychological and social elements. Social workers use group work as another technique. This is a method of working with people in groups of two or more persons to help them. A third technique commonly used by social workers is community organization. This is to organize a group which focuses on the needs of a community.

Jesus manifested many techniques of helping people. He worked with people on a one-to-one relationship. Look through the gospel accounts of Jesus' ministry and one can see snapshot after snapshot of Jesus dealing with one person. He dealt with a pillar of the religious establishment, Nicodemus; with a loose moral woman at Jacob's well; and with a rich young ruler. Also, Jesus used group therapy. Throughout the gospels, Jesus utilized the twelve apostles for bringing about changes in personal and group living. Through transformed people Jesus worked to change an entire city.

What are the techniques that Jesus uses to help people? God deals with the inward being. The Lord represents the supreme social worker. The social worker can only work to change the circumstances of needy people. They can deal with symptoms. They may provide food, read to the illiterate, or take children from the slums for a weekend of pleasure. They may provide help for the homeless, jobless, sick, hungry, or aging. Social workers deal mainly with symptoms. One serious drawback is that they cannot change the inward person.

Jesus is the unusual social worker. He deals with the circumstances, but his technique goes deeper in that he changes character. Jesus fed five thousand on a mountain side near the Sea of Galilee, but he later spoke of the Bread of life. This would appease the deepest and strongest appetities of living. Jesus befriended Mary Magdalene when others shunned her, but he also changed the innermost being of her life. Jesus did a casework with the woman at the well. He listened as any effective social worker would. Yet, the Lord wanted her to center her life with him. Through her faith she was transformed from within her being. Jesus could have given lectures to Zacchaeus about the needs of poor people, but it would have had little effect. When Zacchaeus trusted the Lord, then from a changed heart he gave one-half of his goods to the poor. Mere benevolent social services can help a person in austere circumstances, but only the Lord can change the person.

What a great picture of God as he responds to a society in crisis! God does not respond in disgust to people's plight. Neither does the Lord reprimand them for their needs. He does not seek information on how and why they got in such a bad circumstance. No, Jesus explained God as a God who responds to human needs with the predominant desire and the unique method of changing their character.

God uses the technique of using a transformed individual to transform society. A changed person can relate and respond properly to human needs. Uniting a person's life to Jesus Christ leads to an obedience to the Father's will. The person who loves God will love his fellow human beings. The changed individual is in the process of becoming like the heavenly Father. Consequently, the Christian relates to the issues of daily life because he has God's nature within him.

God works through the church to build fellowship. This is the practice of love and concern by those who share a common allegiance to Christ. The church forgives and helps one another. They refuse to erect social and pretentious barriers. They pray for each other, strengthen one another, restore one another, and share material possessions. God put the church on earth to be a colony of heaven. No one has greater concern for the issues of life than God's people. They are concerned about family life, daily work, race relations, citizenship, morals, concerns which destroy human dignity such as drug abuse, gambling, and pornography. The church serves as God's salt, God's light, and God's leaven to help stabilize the structure of society. It is God's technique to help interpersonal competence and social functioning. Only God has the technique to help a needy world.

The Resources to Rehabilitate

Effective social work involves a program of rehabilitation. The social worker attempts to make it possible for the client to face his problem and to help the client help himself. Contrary to what people may think, the social worker does not just dispense immediate and temporary relief. He endeavors to help a person with self-understanding and his relations to others and to tap his own and community resources to solve the problem. Social workers labor under the premise that people have ego strengths to solve their own problems. For example, the social worker is concerned with more than the distribution of bread. They will feed the hungry, but they will seek to utilize various resources in teaching the person to earn bread.

God is infinitely more interested than immediate relief from a need. The Lord wants the individual to relate redemptively within society. Jesus made known the great ways of the Lord during his earthly ministry. Looking closely into the social work of Jesus, we see that Jesus was far more a dispenser of bread or an easer of disease and handicaps. The Lord gave people the resources to have a healthy self-concept and to have a useful part to fulfill in society.

How does Jesus enable people to live in society? The Lord gives the therapy of a new dynamic. Let us look at scenes throughout the life of Jesus and see how he gave a new dynamic to helpless people. To a paralyzed man healed by the Master, the Lord said: "Arise, and take up thy bed, and go thy way into thine house" (Mark 2:11). These words of Jesus suggest that not only did Jesus heal the paralyzed man, but he gave him the dynamic to walk. When Jesus drove the demons from the man who lived in Gadara, he gave the man an inward dynamic to live free from evil powers. When Jesus called disciples, he gave them dynamic to execute his orders. Wherever we see the Lord in the gospels helping with problems, we see those helped possessed with a dynamic to live a new kind of life.

Jesus promised his followers an enabling power for the living of life. "But ye shall receive power, after that the Holy Ghost is come upon you" (Acts 1:8). "And I will pray the Father, and he shall give you another Comforter, that he may abide with you for ever" (John 14:16). God lives within every believer. This means that the child of God possesses God's power to enable him to evaluate problems or to withstand temptations. God working by his Spirit gives power to the believer.

Several years ago an interesting article appeared in *National Geographic* about the Amazon River. The article related some interesting facts about the great river. The river has a greater volume of water than the total of eight other largest rivers on earth. It discharges sixty times as much water as the Nile River in Egypt. When running full, the Amazon dumps eight trillion gallons of water into the Atlantic each day. This amounts to twenty times the amount needed to supply the power for the United States.[2] God has the power needed to supply what every human being needs.

God rehabilitates people with the powerful dynamic of his Spirit. The Lord gives power for holy living. We cannot produce the Christ-like qualities, but God gives us the power of his Spirit to be Christlike. The Lord gives the dynamic for endurance under any circumstances. We cannot meet the vicissitudes and the assaults of life without the dynamic of God's Spirit. What a great God we worship! He has power to rehabilitate us for the living of these days.

The Lord also gives the therapy of diversion. A social worker often uses a type of diversion therapy to help people with their problems. Arts and crafts are used frequently by psychiatric social workers to turn the client in a new direction. Often social workers encourage the client's involvement in new or redirected activities.

God utilizes the therapy of diversion in helping the needs of people. He encourages people to turn from the self-centered life to the self-giving life-style. Listen to the Lord's therapy: "For whosoever will save his life shall lose it; but whosoever shall lose his life for my sake and the gospel's, the same shall save it" (Mark 8:35). Jesus turned the attention of the self-centered, greedy tax collector from self-concern to a ministry for others. The problems of our day could be solved if people followed the therapy of the Master. Every economic problem would be solved if people lived for what they could do for others and not for what they could get for themselves. The divisions which tear nations or other groups of people asunder would not occur as frequently if the desire of every person was to serve others. When Jesus spoke of the therapy of diverting your attention from yourself to others, he laid the foundation for a great society and a happy world.

Now when you read your New Testament look for the portrait of God as the social worker. It will give you a greater dimension and insight into the true and living God. This portrait will cause you to see how much he cares for you.

14.
The Appetite Appeaser

Modern educators place a strong emphasis on visual aids. It is a means of using sight as a chief medium in aiding learning. Many subjects can be explained more effectively with the use of charts, maps, models, drawings, or film projectors. In the seminary where I teach, a leading educator came to talk with our faculty and administration about some managerial concepts. For forty-five minutes the lecturer spoke about complicated concepts of institutional management and promotion. I did not understand his lecture, and most of my colleagues confessed their lack of comprehension. After this first lecture, the educator utilized several slides and series of overhead transparencies to visualize the concepts he talked about in his lecture. The visual presentation clarified the complicated concepts, and both the group and I responded with more understanding to the lecturer's ideas.

God is the unique Lord. No one can tell all about God. He has revealed the complexity of his nature so that people may get various glimpses of him. Jesus came to earth and explained many insights into God's nature and character. He used various means to give people a glimpse of God. He preached sermons, taught with parables and word metaphorical language which would be understandable. Some of the metaphorical snapshots which the Master used of the Lord was the light of the world, the door, the Vine, the rock, the great High Priest, the bright morning star, and numerous other visual aids.

Once when Jesus was in the area of Galilee, he used a memorable occasion to teach about God. He fed five thousand people with five loaves of bread and two small fish. This small quantity of food was multiplied so miraculously by Jesus that it satisfied the hunger of a fainting multitude. This deed demonstrated God's compassion and love for needy people. After the miracle, Jesus withdrew from the multitude to a quiet spot across the Sea of Galilee.

Jesus decided to use the miraculous incident of the feeding of the five thousand and teach the people about God. Using the object lesson of bread, he said, "I am the bread of life: he that cometh to me shall never hunger; and he that believeth on me shall never thirst" (John 6:35). Jesus compared the hungry multitude with the spiritual hunger of human beings. With the illustration of bread, Jesus tells a great truth about God. The hunger of the human situation is ended when we know Christ. Restless, searching human beings can be at rest and satisfied with the Lord. Jesus taught that God is the real spiritual bread that can satisfy the hunger of a lifetime. "My Father giveth you the true bread from heaven. For the bread of God is he which cometh down from heaven, and giveth life unto the world" (John 6:32–33). Jesus told some great truths about God with the visual use of some bread.

The Essence of Life

Jesus used the incident of feeding the five thousand as a visual aid to teach the lesson that God is the essence of life. In Jesus' day bread was considered the staff of life. Failure to eat bread meant death. Eating daily bread meant life. Therefore, bread was equated with the essence of life.

Bread was the chief food in Israel. The poor made the bread from barley flour with various other ingredients. The rich used wheat to make their bread. Yet, the rich and the poor both had some type of bread as a part of their diet every day. They could not think about life without bread. It is no wonder that these people associated bread with the essence of life. Jesus used this concept to teach that God was as necessary for living as their daily bread. God is absolutely essential for life.

Jesus said, "I am the bread of life" (John 6:35). With this expression Jesus identified himself with the nature of God. The Greek verb translated "I am" was used often as a connective. The predicate amplified and explained the nature of the subject. In this case the "I" refers to Jesus, and the bread describes something of the essence and character of the Lord. Jesus dared to say that he is the essence of life.

God makes life. Scientists for years have studied the marvelous fact of life. Telling exactly what life is and explaining where life originated are two hard exercises. James asked the question, "For what is your life:" (Jas. 4:14). No adequate scientific or philosophical answers have yet been given to that question. Through the years people have told many interesting facts about life: "Life is great!" "Life is hard." "Life is brief." But no one has been able to tell the essence of life.

Jesus said, "I am the bread of life" (John 6:35). It is significant that Jesus used the phrase "of life." This helps us to understand something about the essence of life. The word Jesus used for life is the Greek word *zoe*. This means a special kind of life. It refers to the fact that God made up the ingredients which comprise life.

One of the greatest truths a person can learn about God is that he is the maker of life.

God is also the meaning of life. The creation story tells us that God is the maker of life, but the redemption story tells us that God is the meaning of life. Creation tells us that God made our span of days, but God also put meaning and significance into the span of life. Using the visual aid Jesus told people what makes life meaningful. Life is not made meaningful by mere existence. The essence of real living is the "bread of God is he which cometh down from heaven, and giveth life unto the world" (John 6:33). The life about which the Lord spoke is far more than existence during a span of years. It is a meaningful life—happy, significant, full of purpose, exciting.

Jesus saw a multitude of people that he fed with five loaves and two fish. He made life for them for a day. But the Master wanted to give them more than bread, he wanted to give them real life. Many people are caught in the flow and quickness of life without any sense of meaning. They resemble something of the feeling of Bonnie in the movie *Bonnie and Clyde*. Bonnie had enjoyed the life of bank robbing until she said, "I thought we were going somewhere, but we are just going." With the bread, Jesus tells us that God is the maker and meaning of that which we call "life."

The Support of Life

Jesus gave another truth about God by the figure of the bread. Jews in ancient Palestine used bread as a support of life. It was that substance which kept life going. People ate bread in order to sustain and support their life. Bread is a substance without which life cannot keep on going. The visual aid of the bread gives us the insight that God not only makes the essentials of life but he supports life.

God provides the necessities of life. Bread in ancient Palestine was often used as synonym for a meal or food. Bread then would mean a necessity of life. It is not a luxury. It is an absolute necessity for the support of life. Jesus said, "I am the bread of life." He communicates the truth that God provides for the necessities of life.

To amplify more about the idea of bread, Jesus used the Old Testament story of the manna in the wilderness. The

Israelites escaped from the Egyptians only to fall prey to an inhospitable desert. God did not withdraw support from the Israelites. The Lord gave the people bread to eat each morning and flesh to eat each evening. For forty years God supported the Israelites with the gift of this bread. The bread from heaven was to satisfy the hunger of the Israelites, but it was sent to teach the lesson that the people should rely upon the providence of God. The Israelites were taught to trust God for his support of their life.

Jesus referred to this episode in Israel's history. He taught that God supported the necessities of Israel during forty years of wilderness wandering. He implied that because he is the Bread of life, he can support us in the necessities of life.

All through the Bible the various portraits of God confirm his providence. Look through the Old Testament, and you will see how God maintained the necessities of his people. The psalmist said, "The Lord is my shepherd; I shall not want" (Ps. 23:1). This means that the shepherd would make all the needful provisions for his flock. The Shepherd's care encompasses everything pertaining to the welfare of the sheep. This idea communicates the concept of God as the provider for his people, and all their real needs will be supplied.

Look in the New Testament and see how Jesus explained God. He taught us to pray, "Give us this day our daily bread" (Matt. 6:11). Paul conceived of God with providence. "My God shall supply all your need" (Phil. 4:19). God is one who "worketh all things after the counsel of his will." God actually cares for the necessities of our lives. Just as bread supplies our daily necessities for living, so the Lord provides the essential necessity for living.

God provides the strength for life. Bread gives strength. It enables us to meet the necessities and challenges of each day. Often I get tired and lack energy. But when I have a good meal, I gain my strength again. Why? Because the strength and energy that was in the food has passed into me and has become my strength. It has made me a stronger and better person.

Jesus gave us the insight that God gives us the strength we need. When our vigor and energy is exhausted, we can appropriate God's strength. His strength makes our strength, being able to be and do what apart from him we could not do or be.

Throughout the Bible, God is portrayed as one who gives strength. To exhausted wilderness wanderers, Jehovah gave daily manna which was turned into energy. The psalmist caught a glimpse of God's strength, "He watereth the hills from his chambers: the earth is satisfied with the fruit of thy works. He causeth the grass to grow for the cattle, and herb for the service of man: that he may bring forth food out of the earth: And wine that maketh glad the heart of man, and oil to make his face to shine, and bread which strengtheneth man's heart" (Ps. 104:13–15). Isaiah saw a glimpse of the strengthening power of God for a distressed people, "Fear thou not; for I am with thee: be not dismayed; for I am thy God: I will strengthen thee; yea, I will help thee; yea, I will uphold thee with the right hand of my righteousness" (Isa. 41:10).

God does not strengthen us by removing life's burdens and anxieties. There is no portrait of God in the Bible as an external factor who enters our situation like a celestial porter to carry our baggage. God works inside us like bread. He strengthens us for our burdens and in our anxieties.

Matthew Arnold wrote his famous poem about meeting a preacher in the worst London slum:

> 'Twas August, and the fierce sun overhead
> Smote on the squalid streets of Bethnal Green,
> And the pale weaver, through his windows seen
> In Spitalfields, look'd thrice dispirited.

I met a preacher there I knew, and said:
'Ill on o'erwork'd, how fare you in this scene?'
'Bravely!' said he: 'for of late have been
Much cheered with thoughts of Christ, the living
bread.'

God is the living bread. What a great glimpse into God's nature and action! He provides for life's necessities, and he strengthens in life's daily problems.

The Gratification of Life

Jesus gave another truth about God with the illustration of bread. A distinctive quality about bread is that it is a daily necessity. You can eat bread in the morning, but by noon you need more bread. Americans eat three meals a day. Often when we eat an enormous meal, we think we will never be hungry again, but we are. Bread has the quality of temporary satisfaction. Each meal satisfies us, but it only lasts for a short time of gratification.

Jesus claimed to be the adequate appetite appeaser. He said, "I am the bread of life: he that cometh to me shall never hunger; and he that believeth on me shall never thirst" (John 6:35). What a statement! Jesus said those who opened their life to the Lord would never hunger again. Moses gave the people temporary relief from hunger, but Jesus gives permanent gratification for life.

People are looking for something or someone who can gratify their deep hunger. Some say, "You cannot be satisfied." One pessimistic writer says, "I have seen everything that is done under the sun; and behold, all is vanity and a striving after wind" (Eccl. 1:14, RSV). Many are hungry for inward gratification—unfulfilled yearnings—hopes deminished—dreams shattered—bodies fatigued—minds disturbed—pockets empty—eyes vacant—boredom of days. They want to be satisfied.

God gratifies because he gives direction to life. The people who ate the bread which he miraculously multiplied sought him for bread only. The direction of their lives involved another meal. They had their bread for one day, and the next day they wanted another handout of bread. Jesus disclosed that God is not the God who looks out for man's temporal satisfaction. He desires a deeper direction for life. Jesus warned the seeker, "Verily, verily I say unto you, Ye seek me, not because ye saw the miracles, but because ye did eat of the loaves, and were filled. Labor not for the meat which perisheth, but for that meat which endureth unto everlasting life, which the Son of Man shall give unto you: for him hath God the Father sealed" (John 6:26–27).

Faith in Jesus Christ provides a direction for life. It means that one does not have to expend their energy in constant search for a gratifying direction for their lives. William James, the famous professor at Harvard, wrote to a friend in January of 1868: "All last winter . . . I was on the continual verge of suicide . . ." [1] The direction of James' life was changed when he turned to the Lord. His pessimistic search of life was ended when Christ gave him a direction for his life.

To trust in God means the end of a search for life's direction is ended. Jesus said, "I am come that they might have life, and that they might have it more abundantly" (John 10:10). The purpose of the human race is to know the Lord and to follow him forever.

God gratifies because he gives us the dimension of life. Did Jesus mean to tell us that when we open our lives to God that we would never have any problems? Does it mean that our lives would be free of struggle and problems? Will life be crowned with the spectacular or fantastic? Jesus did not give an idea that life would be an escape and relief from problems.

God gives us a dimension or perspective of living when we open our lives to him. Dietrich Bonhoeffer knew about the living satisfying bread. The Nazi Gestapo imprisoned him, but during his incarceration he sustained his trust in God. The Lord gave him both a dimension for life and for death. When enemies led him to execution, Bonhoeffer said to his friends, "This is the end. For me the beginning of life." [2]

Victor Frankl, the Austrian psychiatrist, spent some harrowing years in Auschwitz and other German concentration camps. From his atrocious experience he concluded that a person who has a reason for living can endure any circumstances. Frankl is convinced that a person finds meaning in life "to the extent to which he commits himself to something beyond himself, to a cause greater than himself." [3]

When a person opens his life to the Lord, he has a special dimension for living. It means with all the struggles and problems, God has provided an inward gratification. Outward conditions and circumstances may not be what we wish, but the living bread gratifies our life.

Hungry human beings can catch a great glimpse of God. He is the Bread of Life. He is the living bread. If any person eats this bread, he will live meaningfully now and forever.

15.
The
Freedom-Giving Father

Many people possess and cherish favorite snapshots or portraits of their father. My wife takes special delight in a portrait of her father. It is a pose of him sitting in his favorite chair with his pipe in his hand and a pleasant expression on his face. Often I have heard my wife say: "That's my favorite picture of Daddy. It looks just like him." Though I do not have a large portrait of my father, I cherish many interesting and sentimental snapshots of him. Our family has photographed him through many years and in numerous situations. We have pictures of him as a baby, high school days, his time in the Navy, poses of him in his work, snapshots of fishing results, and family photos. Of all the numerous snapshots with the variety of poses, I have my favorite picture of my father. It is one of him standing in front of his business. This pose captured his natural countenance and expression, and it also represented his life's vocation.

The Bible contains numerous poses of the heavenly Father. You can easily see that my favorite portrait of God is framed in Luke 15. From this one picture you can learn many interesting truths about the nature and character of God. Looking closer at this beautiful portrait has brought me numerous insights about the Lord. Stop and look closer into the picture and see if you cannot get another glimpse of God. The younger son requested his inheritance from the father. According to Jewish law the father was bound to leave two-thirds to the elder son and one-third to the younger

(Deut. 21:17). It was not uncommon for a father to divide his estate before he died. Look at an interesting pose of this father. Can you catch a glimpse of him handing the inheritance to the younger son? I can. It gives me an insight into the Lord. This gives me a portrait of a heavenly Father who gives me the power to choose my way in life. Under this portrait, there is the caption—"The Freedom-Giving Father."

What a tremendous portrait of God! He is not the manipulator. He is not the fatalistic foreordainer. God is portrayed all throughout as the freedom giver. He has never made people respond in a way they did not want to respond. He did not make Adam or Eve stay away from the forbidden fruit. Neither did the Lord or anyone else make them take the fruit. God called Abraham out of Ur of the Chaldees, but he did not force him away. Go through the Old Testament and look at the great God who called and invited but did not coerce. Look at the gospel narratives. Jesus called people to follow him, but he would not force them. Some followed the Master, and he worked in their lives. Others rejected the Savior, but he did not call them back and reduce his demands or coerce commitment from them.

All through the Bible God is portrayed as the freedom-giving father. This aspect of God's nature is made sharper in Jesus' story of the man with two sons recorded in Luke 15. The father could have demanded the boy to stay home. He could have prohibited him from going to the far country. He allowed him freedom—a freedom to live responsibly or to live rebelliously away from the father's house. From this particular pose numerous insights about the heavenly Father catch our attention.

God Elects for Salvation

One insight can be easily seen from the picture of the father giving a son his inheritance. It is the idea of the election of the heavenly Father. The father in this simple story did not choose one boy for the far country and the other son to stay home. Nothing in this story gives the idea that the father fixed the distances of either son. Nevertheless, we can decipher from the story that the father chose both boys prior to their choice to live as responsible children. This gives us an insight about the election of the heavenly Father.

God elects according to his personhood. Each time we see God in the Bible it is with a personal portrait and not with some impersonal flash cards displaying mere words: holiness, righteousness, love. God is more than mere words. He is an infinite person, rich in all moral attributes. He is the eternal Father. Therefore, one should not study the will of God or the election of God apart from the revelation of himself as a person. This would prevent many distorted ideas about the true and living God. Never think of God's attributes outside of the picture of a father. Put all of God's traits and works in the context of the "Heavenly Father."

Looking at flash cards of God's attributes has led some to inadequate caricatures of God. In emphasizing the mere will of God some assert that God foreordained some men to eternal life for the exhibition of his love, and others to eternal death for the exhibition of his justice. Those with this concept claim that God created human beings for either salvation or destruction. This is due to the fact that people conceive of God's "mere will" apart from his character. In no place does the Bible teach that God has elected some for condemnation. God wills that none should perish, but that all should live.

God's character is seen in Jesus Christ. Jesus revealed God as the personal and eternal, holy Father of all human beings. All his dealings with human beings displayed that God wanted nothing but the best for every person. No one can look at Jesus' explanation and revelation of the heavenly Father and see a human despot arbitrarily choosing the destiny of people. He is a heavenly Father who elects or chooses people for a great purpose which accords with his character. The father of the two sons acted and reacted to them in accordance with his character. There was no hint of an "impersonal will."

The New Testament pictures that behind anyone's salvation is the initiative of God in election. This rules out any boasting on man's part. Also, the Bible teaches that behind man's damnation is not a cruel God but man's sin and neglect of the true and living God.

God elects according to his personal purpose. God has elected people for a purpose. Think about the father of the two boys. He undoubtedly had a purpose for them. He wanted them to have a good relationship with them; and he wanted them to have a good relationship with each other.

Looking through the Bible at the various poses of God yields the conclusion that God elects as many as possible for salvation. He seeks to save everyone. The purpose of God is the salvation of the world, not the condemnation. When he elected Abraham, God said, "And in thee shall all the families of the earth be blessed" (Gen. 12:3). God placed the Jews in a strip of land located at the crossroads of the world. Later in Israel's history, they were dispersed in all directions. Think of how God sent his Son during the zenith of the Roman Empire. Add to this the universality of the Greek language, and you get the picture of God seeking the multitudes. The apostle Paul preached throughout Asia Minor, Greece, and Rome to Jews and Gentiles alike. All through the Bible the portrait of God's electing grace is encompassed on an ever-widening attitude. Nowhere do we see a portrait of a God trying to elect as few as possible.

The purpose of God for human beings is salvation not damnation. No one can produce any clear picture from the Bible of God willing that any person be lost. Often people use the word "predestination" on a flash card and give the wrong impression of God. The word translated "predestination" appears four times in the New Testament (Acts 4:28; Rom. 8:29–30; 1 Cor. 2:7; Eph. 1:5,11). These references have to do with God's purpose for mankind, namely salvation. Of course God's purpose is not always executed by human beings. Therefore, in the New Testament the opposite of election is nonelection but a person's rejection of God's salvation.

God Makes People Free

Another amazing glimpse into God's nature can be seen in the father and his two sons. It is the fact that the father gave freedom to his boys. He allowed one to get his inheritance early and to go to the far country. The father did not try to make the boy stay home. Furthermore, the father allowed the older boy to stay home and complain about conditions. This is a beautiful portrait of the heavenly Father who made people free to choose their way of life and their destiny.

God treats people as human beings. God made humans as moral beings, equipped with the power of choice. Studying the creation account gives an insight into the kind of God portrayed in the Bible. God made a beautiful universe. He made human beings with an amazing uniqueness. God did not choose to make puppets to manipulate. Instead, he chose to make man in his image with the capability to think, to reason, to understand, and to make decisions.

God did not make robots to be controlled from some heavenly computer. God is not portrayed as a computer operator coercing people into life-styles and destinies. One of the great characteristics that God placed in human beings is freedom. This means a person determines life. Man is not a being whose actions are all predetermined for him by external forces. Man's actions in the final analysis are determined from within. Freedom excludes compulsion from without. The acts of a free being are his own acts.

The father did not confine either boy to life at home. The father did not manipulate the boys. He treated them as human beings. He allowed both boys the opportunity of deciding to remain at home or to go to the far country. To force the boy to stay or to lock him in his room would have been treatment akin to an animal not a human. God doesn't treat us like a dog and chain us. He doesn't treat us like a cow and fence us in. He doesn't treat us like a puppet. He is not a pet keeper or a great manipulator. He is a father who treats his creation as human beings, capable of deciding.

God gives himself over to whatever choice people make. No greater pose of God can be seen than when the father handed over the one-third inheritance to the son. Probably the father knew what his son wanted to do. The father also knew the distress and disappointment of the far country. But he did not withold. Instead he gave the boy the inheritance to go to the far country.

The Bible pictures God as one who is willing for a person to do as he pleases. If one rebels, God will give the person over to this rebellious nature. This is a granting of a freedom which actually leads to bondage. The boy left home thinking he was free. He later found that the life he had chosen was one of bondage. God is such a freedom-giving Father that he will allow a person to destroy himself. Yet, one must always remember that this destruction is one which results as a willful rejection of the heavenly Father's will.

The Bible pictures God as one who does not make people have faith. But it does picture the Lord as one who makes people who trust him. The great god unites with those of faith and begins the marvelous work of regeneration. The more people open their lives in free choosing the more God enters their lives and the more they know of him. God is one who gives himself over to whatever you decide. If you rebel, he gives himself over in wrath. If you trust him, he gives himself over in a righteous activity in your life.

God Frees Bound People

The picture of God in the parable is not completed with a boy abusing his freedom to leave home. The story continues with the account of a beautiful homecoming, complete with a feast, shoes, and a ring. A boy had been bound in the bondage of selfishness. With his decision to return home, he had to renounce his selfish ambitions and return to his father. The amazing trait of the father is that the father accepted the boy back. This is what God does: He releases bound people and makes them responsible children in his family.

God frees bound people. The boy found himself in the tragic bondage of the far country. His notion of liberty was the absence of restraint. Actually there is no such thing as complete freedom. Freedom always has to operate within limits. Stars cannot be free to travel any course they choose. They are free to travel in a course. The boy could not have complete freedom. For him to really be free it meant he had to live as a responsible son. The boy imagined that freedom was in himself. The experience in the far country taught him where real freedom was. Later, the boy acknowledged that there was more freedom with the father's slaves than his life in the far country.

The Bible gives us picture after picture of the God who seeks to free bound people. The Lord called Abraham to be a great nation so that this nation could reach people battered and bruised in bondage to themselves. One of the greatest events in Israel's history was "the Exodus." Historically, it represented the people's deliverance from Egyptian bondage. But Jewish prophets and poets later applied and compared this event to God's release of people from spiritual bondage. Alan Walker in his book *Jesus the Liberator,* sees the life and ministry of Jesus as being one of liberation. Walker says that Jesus frees enslaved man from loneliness, violence, sexual abuse and perversion, greed, and even death. He goes on to say throughout this book that man will continue to search and to call freedom by many names, but when a person encounters Jesus Christ, then he will be truly free. All through the Bible, God is pictured as one who frees bound people.

God binds released people. The boy came home and exchanged freedoms. He exchanged a freedom which led to bondage for a bondage that led to freedom. The father did not accept the boy's repentance and release him from the demands of household responsibilities or from his brother. The father treated the boy as a son, and this boy was to live as a responsible son. He was no longer free to do as he pleased. He already tried that way. He wanted to be made a captive to the father, and then he knew he would be free.

People who have been set free from the bondage of sin get a great glimpse of God. They see a God whose authority it would have been better not to have rejected. They rejoice that the Lord is so loving that he releases them from the bondage. They see God not as a tyrannical despot but as a Father who wants the best for his children. They do not mind living under the authority of the Lord. He demands the best from their lives. Perhaps my greatest insights into God have come to me as a result of seeing why the Father commands me or why he prohibits me from some things. His commands result in my betterment and in the good of others. His prohibitions are not binding and keeping me from good. Instead his negations are the best for my life and for the good of others. Study the commands and the "Thou shalt nots" of the Bible, and you will see a portrait of a Father who wants what is best for you.

16.
The Thirst Quencher

The advertising experts know how to attract people into buying products. They appeal to the basic needs and desires of an individual. Vance Packard in his book entitled *The Hidden Persuaders* makes an incisive investigation into the various techniques which advertisements use to motivate people. Various advertisements appeal to natural appetites, and advertisers seek to convince and persuade people that certain products will satisfy these cravings. Studying the psychological makeup of modern advertising would be an interesting study of the inner desires and needs of an individual.

Think about the number of advertisements which directs its attention to your desire for food or drink. Knowing that the majority of Americans have an overworked food desire, advertisers appeal to this interest. You hear about two all-beef patties, special sauce, lettuce, cheese, pickles, onions, on a sesame seed bun. You hear of delicious, mouth-watering steaks served in an exquisite atmosphere. Almost any food advertisement stimulates my already-alive food desire. The hidden persuaders prove their skill when they make me hungry.

Advertisers also demonstrate their effectiveness in appealing to our thirst. Billboards, radio, newspapers, and televisions appeal to the need to quench our thirst. Each time I see a particular soft drink advertisement, I get thirsty. Or when I hear the appeal for the un-cola, I want to join their rebellion and drink this kind of soft drink. Each time I see a particular iced-tea commercial on television, I crave a cool, refreshing glass of tea. Some coffee advertisements also stimulate my taste buds. People make coffee look so refreshing. Advertisement has found a way to appeal to our desires and to persuade us to use their products.

Looking through the Gospels, I see Jesus not as a hidden persuader but the open persuader. He knew the deep needs and the genuine desires of human beings. He appealed openly to people's needs and desires promising satisfaction as a result of faith in him. One of the clearest pictures of God which Jesus gave in the gospels was the thirst quencher.

The portrait of God as the thirst quencher is framed in two scenes in the Gospel according to John. The first scene was at Jacob's well near the town of Sychar. Jesus was traveling from Judaea into Galilee. He became weary with his journey and sat down at the well to rest and refresh himself. As Jesus sat beside the well, a woman came to draw water. Jesus spoke first: "Give me a drink." She turned in astonishment and said: "I am a Samaritan. You are a Jew. You know our differences." But Jesus used the encounter to teach the woman about God. He claimed to be able to quench a thirst which was deep within her life. The Lord said: "But whosoever drinketh of this water that I shall give him shall never thirst; but the water that I shall give him shall be in him a well of water springing up unto everlasting life" (John 4:14).

The second scene is in the Temple in Jerusalem. Jesus was attending the Feast of Tabernacles. This was the eight day Jewish celebration of the time when God's people had been wanderers in the desert before they reached the Promised Land. The worshipers participated in a special ceremony. Each day of the festival, the people came with their willow and palm branches and formed a roof as they walked around the altar. While the people walked, the priest took a golden pitcher and went down to the pool of Siloam and filled it with water. It was brought back to the Temple while the people recited Isaiah 12:3. The priest took the water and poured it on the altar as an offering to God. While this was being done the Hallel (Ps. 113–118) was sung to the accompaniment of flutes by the Levite choir. The entire ceremony was a thanksgiving to God for his provision of water as the Jews traveled through the wilderness. On the last day of the feast, Jesus utilized a dramatic symbol to give a unique portrait of God. He presented himself as the Water of life, the thirst quencher. "If any man thirst, let him come unto me, and drink. He that believeth on me, as the scripture hath said, out of his belly shall flow rivers of living water" (John 7:37–38). With the symbol of water from these two scenes in the gospel we can get several glimpses of God.

God Invites

The portrait of God as the thirst quencher shows God as an inviter. Looking closely at both of the scenes in John causes us to conclude that God invites people to him. Jesus invited the woman to drink of water that would satisfy her and never make her thirst again. Jesus invited a large group of worshipers at a feast to a greater experience of joy in him. In both of these snapshots the feature of God as an inviter comes into sharper focus.

God encourages people to respond to him. There is no hint in the Bible that God is trying to keep anything away from anyone. All through the Bible we can see God urging people to respond to him. He invited Noah into a place of safety. "And the Lord said unto Noah, Come thou and all thy house into the ark; for thee have I seen righteous before me in this generation" (Gen. 7:1). He invited Israel through the prophet Isaiah: "Ho, every one that thirsteth, come ye to the waters, and he that hath no money; come ye buy, and eat; yea, come, buy wine and milk without money and without price" (Isa. 55:1).

When Jesus came to earth he came as an inviter. The Lord said, "Come unto me, all ye that labour and are heavy laden, and I will give you rest" (Matt. 11:28). The Lord told parables which described God's nature as an inviter. In the parable of the marriage feast, the servants invited people on behalf of the king: "All things are ready: come unto the marriage" (Matt. 22:4). The parable depicts the fact that God invited everyone to the festivities of his kingdom. All through the Gospels Jesus invites people. He invites all types of people to follow him.

If you conceive of God as one who does not want human beings, you look at a human drawing not a biblical portrait. The Bible pictures God as the one who moves toward people and invites them to a relationship with him. Jesus revealed the Father's inner disposition when he said: "For the Son of Man is come to seek and to save that which was lost" (Luke 19:10). God came to look for strayed human beings. He wanted to invite people to take their rightful place as obedient children.

God still invites. Through his Holy Spirit, God invites people to open their lives to him. The last inspired word in the Bible is an invitation: "And the Spirit and the bride say, Come. And let him that heareth say, Come. And let him that is athirst come. And whosoever will, let him take the water of life freely" (Rev. 22:17).

God invites people to respond to him because they need him. Jesus requested the Samaritan woman to give him a drink of water because she had a deeper need or thirst. Jesus asked the worshipers in the Temple to believe on him because they had an emptiness. God invites people with a great thirst to have it quenched. Isaiah offered an invitation to the thirsty and to the poverty-stricken. Jesus extended an invitation to those who labored and to those who were heavy laden. In every case where the Lord invited people there was a real need. God is an inviter. This universal thirst is everyone's need for eternal life.

God Satisfies

The portrait of God as the thirst quencher shows him as the abundant satisfier. God invites people because he can gratify the wants and needs of an individual. Jesus' conversation with the Samaritan woman illustrated God's power to satisfy. "If you drink of the water from the well, you will be thirsty again," Jesus said. Jesus added, "Now if you really knew me, you would ask, and I would give you living water." The woman could not understand anyone who could give this kind of satisfaction. Her misunderstanding was caused by thinking on the physical level.

Jesus promised abundant satisfaction to a crowd celebrating the Feast of Tabernacles. If they would respond in faith to Jesus Christ, they would have a different life. There would be an inward satisfaction. Both the scene at the well and in the Temple demonstrates that Jesus is the satisfying thirst quencher.

God satisfies ultimate needs. Within every human being there are various physical desires which call for satisfaction. The hunger and thirst desires are two drives which must be gratified. Jesus compared the intense desires of hungering and thirsting to the spiritual need of a person. Within every human life there is a thirst for something that only God can satisfy. Augustine, the fourth century B.C. theologian, spoke about "our hearts being restless till they rest in Thee." Within every human life there is an ultimate thirst for God. Nothing will satisfy the thirst but a creature's relationship with the Creator. No one can escape from the longing for eternity which God has put in a person's soul.

God satisfies the ultimate needs permanently. Jesus looked at people searching for ultimate satisfaction. As he observed the pursuits, he saw that people sought to satisfy the deep thirsts for God with temporary solutions. People go to the fountain of material possession, financial security, sexual satisfaction, power and prestige, or intellectual attainment. All of these represent legitimate guests of life, but these satisfy the human thirst only for a while. People have to continue drinking more at these fountains expecting satisfaction. Because of the lack of a permanent gratification people experience vague discontent, an unsatisfied longing, and a frantic frustration.

Jesus promised to satisfy the deepest desires of a person, and he pledged that their gratification would be permanent. Jesus promised the Samaritan woman a "well of water, springing up into everlasting life." He promised the worshipers that out of their beings would "flow rivers of living water." There is no need of seeking elsewhere for a fuller satisfaction. God gives eternal satisfaction. Whoever lives with Christ and in Christ has in his life a spring of water perennial and inexhaustible. God brings the deepest kind of happiness. He gives a life far more abundant than anyone else can know.

The thirst of the human soul can only be satisfied by the thirst quencher. God desires to quench the thirst of every human being. He wants to satisfy. "And let him that is athirst come. And whosoever will, let him take the water of life freely" (Rev. 22:17). Horatius Bonar described God's satisfaction:

> I heard the voice of Jesus say,
> "Behold, I freely give
> The living water, thirsty one,
> Stoop down, and drink, and live:"
> I came to Jesus, and I drank
> Of that life-giving stream;
> My sould was quench'd, my soul revived,
> And now I live in Him.

God Blesses

The portrait of God as the thirst quencher shows God as one who blesses life. If people allow God to enter their lives, he will satisfy them and in turn make them a blessing to the lives of others. Look at the scene again at the well of Sychar. Jesus wanted the woman to commit her life to him. She did, and she became a blessing to the Samaritan community.

God blesses the lives of others through changed lives. The Samaritan woman's thirst for life had been assuaged in Jesus Christ. The Samaritan community took note of the change in her life. "And many of the Samaritans . . . believed on him for the saying of the woman, which testified, 'He told me all that ever I did' " (John 4:39). An entire neighborhood was blessed and attracted to the Messiah by the transformation of one woman.

Read through the Gospels and learn how Jesus changed the lives of people: Peter, James, John, Matthew, Thomas, a Samaritan woman, a Canaanite woman, Zacchaeus, and many others. Read further into these stories of character changes, and you will learn that Jesus blessed the lives of others through these transformed people. When living water quenches thirsty people, it has a tendency to make others thirsty.

The greatest argument for the reality of God is a Christian experience. A coal miner once interrupted John Hutton when he was preaching. He leaped to his feet and led the congregation in singing the doxology. Later the miner explained that he had been a Christian only for some months, and that it was all so gloriously different that he could not sit still in his place. He said, "I was a bad lot; I drank; I pawned the furniture; I knocked my wife about; and now life is real life, and splendidly worthwhile." The miner was asked how he fared among his fellows down in the pit. He laughed and replied, "Today they asked me, 'You don't seriously credit that old yarn about Jesus turning the water into wine?' " To which, I replied: "I know nothing about water and wine, but I know this, that in my house Christ has turned beer into furniture; that is a good enough miracle for me!"

God blesses the lives of others by overflowing lives. Look again at the scene of the Temple. On the last day of the feast, Jesus said: "If any man thirst, let him come unto me, and drink. He that believeth on me, as the scripture hath said, out of his belly shall flow rivers of living water" (John 7:38). Jesus promised to bless lives from the source of satisfied lives. God will pour out his Spirit upon those who receive him, and the blessed will be a strength and inspiration to others. The Spirit-filled and the empowered life has an outflow to others. The believer becomes a channel of blessing to others. Having drunk of the Water of life, the one with the assuaged thirst goes to tell others where they might have their thirst quenched.

One of the greatest pictures of God in the gospel is that of the thirst quencher. It portrays the Lord as the one for whom the world longs. God can satisfy the deepest longings of the human heart. Those who are satisfied by the thirst quencher become themselves channels of spiritual blessings. God's truth and grace will flow through them so that other souls can be satisfied.

Notes

PREFACE

1. Elbert C. Knudson, *The Doctrine of God* (New York: Abingdon Press, 1930), p. 206.

CHAPTER 2

1. William Marsden, *Book of Classic English Poetry* 600-1830. Compiled by Edwin Markham (New York: William H. Wise and Company, 1934).
2. Oscar Cullman, *Christ and Time: The Primitive Christian Conception of Time and History*. Translated by Floyd V. Filson. Revised Edition (Philadelphia: The Westminster Press, 1964), p. 49.

CHAPTER 4

1. Alfred Plummer, *A Critical and Exegetical Commentary on the Gospel According to St. Luke* in the *International Critical Commentary* (New York: Charles Scribner's Sons, n.d.), p. 371.
2. W. T. Conner, *Christian Doctrine* (Nashville: Broadman Press, 1937), pp. 18-21.
3. Quoted in William M. Taylor, *The Parables of Our Saviour* (New York: Doubleday, Doran and Company, Incorporated, 1929), p. 334.

CHAPTER 5

1. Paul Tournier, *A Doctor's Casebook in the Light of* the Bible. Translated by Edwin Hudson, (London: SCM Press Limited, 1954).
2. William Barclay, *The Gospel of Mark* in the Volumes of *The Daily*

Study Bible Series. Revised Edition (Philadelphia: The Westminster Press, 1975), p. 48.
3. James A. Knight, *Conscience and Guilt* (New York: Appleton-Century-Crafts, 1969), p. 4.
4. Maurice F. Egan, "The Old Violin." *An American Anthology* 1787-1900. Edited by Edmund C. Stedman (New York: Houghton Mifflin Company, 1900).

CHAPTER 6

1. The author used the title of this chapter from Helmut Thielicke, *The Waiting Father: Sermons on the Parables of Jesus.* Translated by John W. Doberstein (New York: Harper and Row, Publishers)
2. Russell L. Mast, *Lost and Found* (Scottsdale, Pennsylvania, 1963), p. 96.

CHAPTER 8

1. Frank Stagg, *New Testament Theology* (Nashville: Broadman Press, 1962), p. 92.

CHAPTER 9

1. Leslie D. Weatherhead, *The Will of God* (New York: Abingdon Press, 1954), p. 13.

CHAPTER 10

1. A. M. Hunter, *The Parables Then and Now* (Philadelphia: The Westminster Press, 1971), pp. 70-73.

CHAPTER 12

1. Adolph Harnack, *The Expansion of Christianity in the First Three Centuries*, Volume I. Translated and edited by James Moffatt (London: Williams and Norgate, 1904), p. 161.
2. Joachim Jeremias, *New Testament Theology. The Proclamation of Jesus.* Volume I. Translated by John Bowden (London: SCM Press,

Limited, 1961), p. 94.

Chapter 13

1. Arthur E. Fink, C. Wilson Anderson, and Merrill C. Conover. *The Field of Social Work*. Fifth Edition (New York: Holt, Rinehart, and Winston, Incorporated), p. 1.

Chapter 14

1. Henry James (ed.), *The Letters of William James* Volume I. (Boston: The Atlantic Monthly Press, 1920), p. 129.
2. Dietrich Bonhoeffer, *Letters and Papers from Prison*. Translated by Reginald H. Fuller and edited by Eberhard Bethge (New York: MacMillan Publishing Company, Incorporated, 1953), p. 14.
3. Victor E. Frankl, "The Will to Meaning," in Paul Tournier et al., *Are You Nobody?* (Richmond: John Knox Press, 1966), pp. 26-27.